Survival Guide
for
New Dads

NICK HARRISON
AND STEVE MILLER

HARVEST HOUSE™ PUBLISHERS

EUGENE, OREGON

Cover design by Garborg Design Works, Minneapolis, Minnesota

SURVIVAL GUIDE FOR NEW DADS
Copyright © 2003 by Nick Harrison and Steve Miller
Published by Harvest House Publishers
Eugene, Oregon 97402

Library of Congress Cataloging-in-Publication Data
  Harrison, Nick.
  Survival guide for new dads / Nick Harrison, Steve Miller.
      p. cm.
  Includes bibliographical references and index.
  ISBN 0-7369-1088-3 (pbk.)
   1.   Fathers — Religious life.   I. Miller, Steve, 1960–   II. Title.
  BV4529.17 .H36 2003
  248.8'421 — dc21   2002014923

Printed in the United States of America

   03   04   05   06   07   08   09   10   / VP-MS /   10   9   8   7   6   5   4   3   2   1

Other Books
by Nick Harrison

*Promises to Keep: Daily Devotions
for Men Seeking Integrity*

*365 WWJD: Daily Answers to
"What Would Jesus Do?"*

His Victorious Indwelling

Magnificent Prayer

Other Books
by Steve Miller

Amazing Mazes for Kids

Bible Trivia for Kids

Memory Verse Games for Kids

A Child's Garden of Prayer
(coauthored with Becky Miller)

C. H. Spurgeon on Spiritual Leadership

What the Bible Says About…
(coauthored with Bob Phillips)

An Invitation from Nick and Steve

Welcome to the wonderful, sometimes wacky world of fatherhood! In the next 18 years (make that longer, if you eventually have more children) God is going to shape you into a totally different type of guy than you've previously been—a *good* kind of different. Along the way, there will be some challenges. There will also be disappointments, goof-ups, tears, and anguish. But those will be far outweighed by the joys, laughter, and good times that will make the fatherhood phase of your life on earth a true delight.

The best way to think about fatherhood is this: God has chosen you for a special assignment. Out of the three billion other men on earth right now, He's chosen *you* to be the father of this particular child who has just erupted into the world. Whether this unique new individual was born to you and your wife or has come into your family through adoption doesn't really matter—*God chose you.*

So are you up the challenge? Think you can cut the mustard? Sure, you can! And here's some help.

We've been fathers for...well, more than a century if you combine the ages of our three sons (Steve) and three daughters (Nick). During those years, we've experienced just about everything from the advent of disposable diapers to the notion that fathers are irrelevant. They aren't. You are needed in the daily job of nurturing your son or daughter for as long as you live. (No, your job isn't over on their eighteenth birthday. Being a father is a lifelong calling and blessing.)

This book, then, is intended to be a survival guide for new dads. Rookies. Greenhorns. Newbies. And we're writing as a pair of dads who have been there, done that. We were once in your shoes, and we've faced the many exhilarations and challenges you're about to experience. Our advice for survival is both spiritual and practical, based on common sense, tradition, and the advice God offers us in the Bible. It also occasionally looks ahead to the years when your child is no longer an infant—years that will, all too soon, be upon you. So many of the things you begin to do as a father now will bear fruit later. A good dad thinks ahead.

Dad, you've got some tremendous new experiences in the years to come. We both wish you the best as you grow comfortably into fatherhood. And may God richly bless your family!

—⚬—

Fearfully and
Wonderfully Made

*I praise you because I am fearfully and
wonderfully made; your works are wonderful,
I know that full well.*

(PSALM 139:14)

If you want to grace that empty wall in your home with a
Picasso—the real thing, of course, not a print—and you want to
get an idea of what you might expect to pay, a portrait done by
this master sold for $23.9 million in the summer of 2002.[1] Or if
you prefer the French Impressionists, there's always Monet. His
work *Waterlilies* sold for a mere $20.1 million that same week.[2]
And if you've been working hard lately and you feel you deserve
something a bit more special, there's the still life by Paul
Cezanne that sold for $60 million at a recent Sotheby's auction.[3]

But there is one exceptionally gifted Master whose works of
art are priceless—so much so that you won't even find them on
the market. However, this artist is unusually benevolent and
finds great pleasure in giving away His masterpieces all over the
world. In fact, if you're a parent, you own at least one of them.

We cannot help but look at a baby and marvel at the deli-
cate complexity of God's handiwork. The graceful swirls on the
skin at the tip of every tiny finger and toe. Skin softer than a
rose petal, yet strong enough to serve as a protective shield.
Eyes, ears, and a nose that are perfectly detailed miniatures yet
every bit as functional and capable as those on a grown-up.

What's truly remarkable is that God produces each masterpiece in complete darkness. They're not rush jobs, either. Not even the most powerful microscope can fully reveal the infinite detail that goes into each of the Master Artist's creations.

From the moment the clock starts ticking at conception, life is already incredibly complex. Millions upon millions of processes are involved in the assembly of a new life, all perfectly orchestrated by the Master Conductor with precision and skill. By day 18, the heart is already beating. At six weeks, brain waves are measurable, and during the second month, the skeleton is formed. At eight weeks, the vital organs are functioning. At nine to ten weeks, a fetus can hiccup and react to loud noises from outside the womb. A little later, we're already seeing facial expressions, including frowns and smiles. At 11 weeks, the baby can breathe, taste, swallow, digest, and sleep. All this in the *first trimester!*

Each child bears the personal imprint of the Master—His brush strokes, His color scheme, His loving attention to detail. And each treasure is given to us freely, delivered into our hands with great pride and joy. Indeed, Psalm 139:14 says it all so perfectly: Your child is fearfully and wonderfully made...by no less that the God of the universe Himself. Marvelous are His works!

Making It Happen—Consider the meticulous care that is given to preserving the works of art that hang on the walls of such museums as the Louvre, the National Gallery of Art in Washington, D.C., and the British Museum. Do you treat and care for your child as the masterpiece he or she is? Take a moment now to thank God for His amazing work in your child...and to commit yourself to providing the very best care you can possibly give.

A Father's Touch

He took a little child and had him stand
among them. Taking him in his arms, he said to them,
"Whoever welcomes one of these little children in my
name welcomes me; and whoever welcomes me does
not welcome me but the one who sent me."

(Mark 9:36-37)

The first time a father holds his new baby, he may feel as though the infant were made of glass. But with practice, that dad is soon holding the infant as comfortably as a football or a briefcase.

Touch is important to a child—starting from the very earliest days. So start the pattern of appropriate touching now, while your child is an infant. Carry him or her often. Hold your baby close to your chest. Let your son or daughter quickly learn your distinct masculine smell and touch.

As the child grows, you will learn new ways of showing affection through the power of your touch, such as "daddy-tuck-me-in-bed" times, pat-on-the-back times for a job well done, and of course, hugs—the expression of affection that will outlast all others. Your child will never be too old for a hug from dad.

Remember these cautions about touching: Sometimes, in anger, perhaps when the baby cries long past your bedtime, you'll be tempted to touch your child with harshness. Beware of such times. Many a young child has learned to *fear* the touch of his or her father, for it has primarily been during times of physical chastisement that the child has known paternal touch. A baby is too young to understand physical discipline—that will come later.

Some children—yes, even babies—have known the horror of their father's touch through unspeakable acts of sexual abuse. The result is often many years of deep inner struggle in an attempt to heal wounds inflicted by dad's misuse of God's gift of parental touching. Respect your child's privacy. Never touch a child at any age in a way that suggests anything other than *parental* affection.

Dad, touching is part of bonding. Feeling the comfort of your touch will help your child know your love.

Making It Happen—The most practical way for your baby to bond with your nearness and touch is for you to hold him or her often. Hold the baby close to you—a newborn can most easily focus on your face from eight to ten inches away. Look your baby in the eyes—studies have shown that an infant's heart rate rises when his or her eyes are focused on a parent's face. Let your fingers become the baby's favorite toys. Soothe his or her hair. This nearness also lets him or her get used to your smell.

And as your young family goes on shopping trips, you can be the one to slip on the baby carrier. Be sure you have a carrier that's comfortable for you, your wife, and your baby. For newborns, the baby is best carried in the front, on your chest. As the child grows, a carrier that fits on your back is more ideal, providing more comfort for you and allowing your now-curious baby to see what's ahead.

Praying for the New Mom

Husbands, love your wives...

(EPHESIANS 5:25)

Who is the most significant person in your life right now?

If you're a husband, the answer should be obvious: your wife. The marriage relationship is the most primary, most intimate human relationship that exists. So it's appropriate when we call our spouse "my significant other."

That raises another question: If your wife is the most significant person in your life, then wouldn't it be appropriate for you to be praying significantly for her? Especially now that she is a new mother? Undoubtedly you've noticed the many changes that have taken place in her life, and one of the best ways you can support her now is through prayer.

Think about it. She needs prayer for strength (your baby's constant need for attention deprives your beloved of her sleep). She needs prayer for discernment (why is the little one crying this time?). She needs prayer as her body continues to adjust to post-pregnancy and breast-feeding. She needs prayer for patience (a fussy baby can easily get on one's nerves!). She needs prayer for wisdom (how can I best rearrange my schedule to meet the needs of my growing family?). These are just a few of the ways you can pray for your wife-become-mother.

—

With that in mind, why not devote a significant portion of your prayer time to lifting your wife's needs and concerns to the Lord? An obvious benefit of praying regularly for your wife is that it will help you to understand her better, to walk in her shoes. You'll come to appreciate the feelings and struggles in her heart as well as the obstacles and trials she faces each day. You'll come to see circumstances from her perspective—which will awaken you to things you've never noticed before.

This is a powerful and meaningful way to enrich your marriage. Walking with your wife as both a marriage partner *and* a prayer partner will not only draw you closer to her, it will also help you place God right where He belongs—at the center of your marriage.

Making It Happen—In the morning as your wife prepares for the day, remember to ask her, "How can I pray for you today?" When you make this a habit, your wife will sense that you genuinely care about her and are interested in her needs. Even more meaningful would be for you to put feet to your prayers by actually giving your wife a helping hand in her areas of need. Start today!

Another way you can encourage your beloved is to get her a copy of *365 Things Every New Mom Should Know* by Linda Danis (Eugene, OR: Harvest House Publishers, 2002).

Every Child a Special Being

All the days ordained for me were written in your book
before one of them came to be.

(PSALM 139:16)

Planet Earth is home to more than six billion people. How many of those six billion consider you an important part of their life? How many of them even know you exist? When you think of your stature in this world in those terms, it makes you feel pretty insignificant, doesn't it?

Now take a moment to consider that 356,000 babies are born each day worldwide. In the United States, the figure is well over 10,000 babies per day. When it comes to sheer numbers alone, it may seem your child is "just another baby." To the U.S. Census Bureau, your little one is just another statistic. But in God's eyes, that's not the case at all! Your child is a very special, one-of-a-kind, lovingly created being.

When we think of God's involvement in our child's life, we tend to think of the fact that God created him or her, and little else. But God's work goes far beyond just the act of creation. Psalm 139:16 says that God planned every detail of every single day of your child's life long before he or she was born: "In Your book they all were written, the days fashioned for me, when as yet there were none of them" (NKJV). God meticulously orchestrated the entirety of your child's existence ages ago! In fact, when it comes to the matter of salvation in Christ, Ephesians 1:4

says that God chose us "before the creation of the world." Though that verse refers to being chosen spiritually by God, still, it indicates that God's involvement in every human's life began in eternity past!

Then there's God's ongoing, everyday care for your child. In Matthew 18:10, Jesus said, "Do not look down on one of these little ones. For I tell you that their angels in heaven always see the face of my Father in heaven." God is ever-watchful, evidently to the point of providing protective angels. In Psalm 139:8-10, King David told God, "If I go up to the heavens, you are there; if I make my bed in the depths, you are there; if I rise on the wings of the dawn, if I settle on the far side of the sea, even there your hand will guide me." God was *constantly* present with David— and the same is true about God and your child.

Long ago in eternity past, then, God planned your baby's entire future. And during the nine months in the womb, your little one was shaped by God's own hand. All through your offspring's life, God's hand will lead and hold him or her.

Wouldn't you say that makes your child pretty special?

Making It Happen—How special do you think your child is to God? How does this knowledge affect the way you view your little one? Before today is over, get together with your wife and baby and take time to say a prayer of thanks to the Lord for His intimate involvement in all of your lives. Thank Him for giving this very special child to you and ask Him to help you love him or her in a way that affirms just how special he or she is.

It's Never Too Early

Pray without ceasing.

(1 Thessalonians 5:17)

We knew he didn't understand a word we were saying. Nor would he understand for many more nights to come. Sometimes he slept through our words. That was okay, too.

Very early in our firstborn son's life, we began a little tradition that came to have a greater impact than we ever expected. We prayed with Keith every night at bedtime. We would hold hands together, bow our heads, and say a brief yet heartfelt prayer. And with our second and third sons, Nathan and Ryan, we started as soon as they came home from the hospital.

Again, they didn't understand our words. But they did feel the warm and caring touch of our hands. And they heard our quiet voices speak in reverence to and dependence upon God as we brought our requests and thanks to Him. We kept the prayers simple, for we knew that in time, understanding would come, and we could have them join in the prayers as well.

Proverbs 22:6 says to "train a child in the way he should go." If there were only one habit we could ever train into our children, we wanted it to be prayer. And as our boys grew older, if the hour was late and we had not yet prayed together, they would come to us and ask, "When are we going to pray?" They *wanted* to pray—there was no need for pressure from us. For them, the day was incomplete without prayer.

It's never too early to make prayer a part of your children's lives. Prayer lets them know that God is very real, that we can talk to Him, and that He will listen to us. When our children hear us express our dependence upon God to meet our needs, they will learn that they can take their needs to Him, too. Through our prayers, our offspring will come to know more about who God is, what He is like, and how they can enjoy a personal relationship with Him.

When you make prayer a natural part of your family life, it's far more likely to become a natural part of your children's lives, too.

Making It Happen—One way to pray with your child is to read prayers from a baby's prayer book. If you don't have one already, buy one and place it near the crib so you can read it together at night. Be sure to close with your own simple prayer as well and to include your child's name in the prayer. Name recognition comes early for little ones and makes the prayer more meaningful to them.

Every Child a Wanted Child

Fear not, for I have redeemed you;
I have summoned you by name; you are mine.

(ISAIAH 43:1)

Is there really such a thing as an "unwanted child"? Not in God's eyes. Every baby is born by God's fiat. No baby is a "mistake." But babies are perceptive. They can quickly sense just how wanted or unwanted they are—and react accordingly. A baby who feels rejected by dad, even in infancy, can carry these feelings into childhood and beyond.

Many dads think of their new status as having merely to do with provision or offering support for mom. But your job specs as dad include much more. And your foremost duty beyond providing the physical necessities of a home and food is that of projecting total acceptance of this new resident in your house.

Right now, examine your feelings about this baby of yours. Does he or she seem like some sort of stranger you must cope with for the next 18 years? Or perhaps you're not quite so aloof. Perhaps you really do love this child with all your heart but are still uneasy about being a father. Will you fail? Will this child grow to love you and respect you? Are you concerned that this little one may be a disguised bundle of future problems, arguments, and estrangements? Are you concerned that even as a well-intentioned father, you and your cuddly newborn may eventually turn into enemies? Perhaps that happened to you and your own father.

It doesn't have to be that way for you and your child. If you are even slightly hesitant to accept your new role—and this new baby—now is the time to abandon forever those feelings, embrace the role of fatherhood, and bond fully with your son or daughter. And let God be the source of that bond.

Making It Happen—Offer a prayer of acceptance for this baby. Thank God for this new life and commit yourself anew to your new role as dad. Perhaps in so doing, you'll find a way to make peace with your own father, if necessary.

The Power of the Written Word

Then the LORD said to Moses, "Write this
on a scroll as something to be remembered...."

(EXODUS 17:14)

I'm not much for keeping journals. I'm a busy man, and I always drag my feet before implementing one more add-on to my life. But a few years ago, some powerful things were happening in our family, most of which my daughters were unaware. And yet I sensed it would be good for them to know what their dad was feeling as I underwent these serious challenges.

Somewhat reluctantly I went to a local office supply store and bought three hardcover notebooks with blank pages inside to use as journals. Inside the front cover of each, I entered the name of one of my three daughters. I knew it would be foolish to vow that I would write something for all three every day or even every week. But I knew I could write a few lines every so often...for instance, when they were undergoing some life changes, such as a new school, a fight with a friend, or a graduation. So I began slowly, writing only when I had something important to say. Several years have passed, and I'm still keeping those "occasional" journals. Sometimes I find myself simply writing of my love for my daughters and relating the current event that prompted my journal entry. Or I try to lavishly praise the girls when they accomplish something memorable (of course, I do this verbally also, not just in the journals). I've also allowed myself to become pretty transparent with the girls on these pages. Perhaps there's a depth of myself that I'm able to share more easily by writing to the girls than by speaking to them. Occasionally, I also tape an especially wonderful Father's Day or birthday card I've received to the pages with my thoughts and thanks for their applause on these special days.

By now, these journals cover quite a few pages. But sometimes months pass between entries. Rarely are there two entries within a week or two of each other—and that's okay. Rather than a legalistic and rigid routine, keeping the journals has been a voluntary exercise in joy.

For some reason, I've not told my daughters about these journals. I suppose I have some fanciful notion that years from now, perhaps when I'm gone, their mother will present these books to them as presents—a way to keep dad's influence and memory alive. But who knows, someday I may simply decide I've kept them long enough and present them to the girls myself.

I have only one regret about these occasional journals—that I didn't begin right away, when my daughters were infants. How I wish I had recorded my feelings at witnessing their birth or the day they took their first steps or uttered their immortal "Da-da."

Guys, go buy one of these journals for your newborn. Keep it handy, where you will see it often and find it accessible for adding a new entry every so often.

Remember, you're not writing a monumental tome like *War and Peace*—this is simply an occasional glimpse into the memories you and your child are building into each other's lives. Keep it simple…but keep it.

Making It Happen—Stop at Staples, Office Depot, or some such store and pick up a blank book. Try to choose one that's colorful and attractive, maybe even "gifty" looking. Your first entry can be about the day you learned your wife was pregnant. Then you might recount the day of the baby's birth and homecoming from the hospital. If the baby's birth was listed in the newspaper's vital statistics page, cut the notice out and tape it in the book.

Then, enter your thoughts as often as you like.

The Family Bed

I will lie down and sleep in peace, for you alone,
O LORD, make me dwell in safety.

(PSALM 4:8)

If you had time to read the many different baby-care books written during the past century, you'd notice how faddish some of them can be. Several decades ago, it was quite the thing for mom to be rendered unconscious while the baby was delivered, for the baby to be put on a "formula" right away (instead of mom's breast milk), and for dad to pace the waiting room floor.

But then doctors began to realize what nature and common sense have said all along: Most moms can handle—and actually prefer—being awake during childbirth. And not surprisingly, it's also been "discovered" that mom's supply of milk is superior to store-bought nourishment. And as for dad…well, not only is he now welcome in the delivery room, in some cases he also is coached to help deliver the baby.

Also falling by the wayside in many families is the foreign concept that babies must be hidden away in another room at night, away from mom and dad. What a surprise to the babies! All day long they're cuddled, hugged, and held near…and then at night they're tucked away by themselves in their own bed. It's as if we expect them to understand that for the next several hours there will be no more tender affection while everyone else tries to sleep. Is it any wonder that babies cry at night, separated from the touch and care of their parents?

Many parents are discovering that it is important to have the baby not only in the same bedroom, but *occasionally* in the same bed. For one thing, it's sure a lot easier for a sleepy mom to nurse the baby without trekking to another room and staying awake while the infant nurses. Many mothers happily report the joy of both mother and baby falling back to sleep in mom and dad's bed, secure, warm, and loved.

It wasn't until recent decades that the new baby or even toddler was banished to a different room for the night. For centuries there was the large bed in which both mom and dad and a child or two slept peacefully together.

Perhaps this sounds unworkable…but it isn't really. It may work better in some situations than in others. But dad, don't discount it. For many parents, *it works!* Such families bond tremendously as children are assured of security and love, even during the night hours.

So dad, *sometimes* it may be best for the baby to be in bed with you and mom. So roll over and give them some room. In fact, you might be your wife's hero if you suggest this solution to the midnight feedings.

Making It Happen—For more information and some good answers to all your objections, you might want to get a copy of *The Family Bed* by Tine Thevenin. Read it prayerfully and with discernment—not everything she suggests is practical for every family or necessarily written from a sound spiritual point of view. Also, many websites exist with good information on this important topic—too many to list. Do a search under "family bed." You'll find lots to think about—and answers to the most common questions or objections.

Coping with Crying

Be kind and compassionate to one another.

(EPHESIANS 4:32)

Many parents will tell you that nothing is more beautiful than an infant adrift in a contented, blissful sleep. He or she looks so peaceful, so innocent…and the sight tugs at your heartstrings. And at the opposite end of the spectrum, nothing is more frustrating than the ear-shattering scream that just won't stop. Sometimes you're able to figure out what your baby wants and bring an end to the crying—what a relief! But sometimes the crying goes on…and on…and on. What can you do?

Remember that your baby is not crying because he or she is upset or uncomfortable with you. Don't take the crying personally, or you may end up getting angry, and that will just make the situation worse. Remember that crying is a baby's main mode of communication, so don't let it frustrate you or make you feel inadequate in your parenting. Rather, look at your child's cries as his or her attempts to communicate with you. In time, you'll learn to tell the difference between different kinds of cries and figure out what it is your baby wants or needs. You'll come to know whether your child is saying, "I'm tired," "I'm hungry," "I need changing," or "These clothes are too stuffy."

Here are some great ways to help a crying baby:

Provide a distraction. Sing, read a story, play with his or her hands, or play with a toy with him or her.

Use a pacifier. It's pacifying for a baby to be able to suck on something—a pacifier, a bottle, or a finger or thumb. He or she can't suckle and cry at the same time.

Carry your baby with you. If your child is in a crib or playpen and won't stop crying, carry him or her in your arms or next to your chest. The warmth and closeness may soothe the little one.

Go for a walk or ride. This really does work for a lot of babies. One year during the Christmas season we discovered quite by accident that our middle son, Nathan, was lulled to sleep during our rides around town to look at Christmas lights. Thereafter, whenever he wouldn't stop crying, we'd go for a short drive and…sure enough, he would soon fall asleep.

Two final tips for those longer crying spells: One, take turns doing duty with your partner. Do 10- to 15-minute shifts. The "off" times will help relieve the stress and restore your energy. And two, don't get in the habit of automatically dumping your baby into your partner's hands every time he or she starts crying. Instead, stick with your child through the hard times while he or she is little, and you will gain a greater confidence for handling the hard times that come as they grow older.

Remember, too, that a crying baby can be a distraction during church services and other public events. For the next year or more, you'll want to sit in an aisle seat near the back of the church when your baby is with you. If the baby fusses, either you or mom can take your little one out of the service until he or she quiets down. Don't assume this is automatically mom's job—unless the crying is from hunger and the baby is still breast-feeding. Sometimes just the motion of walking with the baby for a while will lull the infant to sleep. As much as possible, try to leave the baby home from events such as weddings and funerals. These are solemn occasions, vitally important to those who are attending. An unhappy baby can ruin an otherwise memorable event. Be considerate—either hire a baby-sitter or forego the occasion.

And every now and then, don't forget to *thank* God for the gift of crying. While it may hardly seem a gift, it's a needed form

—

of communication. Without it, we would be much more clueless regarding our little one's needs.

Making It Happen—For a week or two, along with your spouse, keep a diary that records your baby's crying fits—how long he or she cried and, if possible, what caused the crying. After a while, you may see patterns emerge—patterns that help you to know your baby's needs better and, as a result, help reduce the crying incidents in your home.

Real Love

Love is patient, love is kind. It does not envy,
it does not boast, it is not proud. It is not rude,
it is not self-seeking, it is not easily angered,
it keeps no record of wrongs.

(1 CORINTHIANS 13:4-5)

When we hear the word *love,* we tend to think of a special feeling we have for another person—a close friend, a family member, or our spouse. But real love is so much more than that. It goes beyond feelings, emotions, hugs, kisses, and holding hands. Real love is manifest not merely in feelings, but through actions. It's not just spoken, but carried out. Real love—the kind of love God shows to His children—willingly makes personal sacrifices for the benefit of others.

How can we as dads show real love to our little one? In just a few simple words in 1 Corinthians 13:4-5, God reveals His perfect definition of love. Let's take a closer look and consider some possible ways we can apply this definition to our little ones.

Love is patient—When your baby cries, cries, and cries some more, let it become an exercise in cultivating greater patience. See if you can figure out the reason for the crying, and with a heart of compassion, do what you can to soothe your child.

Love is kind—Rather than being satisfied with doing "just enough" to take care of your baby, go the extra mile. Add the extra touches that show him or her you really care.

It does not envy—Don't wish yourself into the shoes of other parents whose babies seem easier to handle. Have a heart of genuine thanks for the child God has given you. God gave you this child because He knew you were the right dad for him or her!

It does not boast, it is not proud—As you carry out your fatherly duties, are you seeking attention or accolades? Or are you perfectly content when only you and God know about your "good deeds"?

It is not rude...it is not easily angered—Do you sometimes find yourself feeling antagonistic toward your child? Ask the Lord to help you replace that with gentleness and kindness.

It is not self-seeking—One of the greatest challenges of becoming a new father is having to set aside your *wants* in order to take care of baby's *needs.* You'll probably read the paper less and golf less. But caring for another life is one of the most noble callings we can ever fulfill—and the rewards last for eternity.

It keeps no record of wrongs—When your child wrongs you, forgive and forget. God's mercies are new every morning (Lamentations 3:22-23); may yours be new every morning as well.

Making It Happen—Go back over 1 Corinthians 13:4-5. With each part of these verses, think of practical ways you can show God's kind of love to your wife. Now that you have ideas for both your child and wife, put them to use!

A Father's Joy

Sons are a heritage from the LORD,
children a reward from him.

(PSALM 127:3)

Though the responsibilities of fatherhood are great, the rewards are even greater. Journalist Joseph A. Breig expressed this well in these words taken from *A Halo for Father:*

> Much is written in poetic praise of motherhood. Little is written in that vein of fatherhood. The father is generally regarded as a kind of noble but weary beast of burden, silently enduring the tedium of providing for his family. Of the rewards of fatherhood almost nothing is said. Yet I suspect that the most gigantic of all human joys are experienced by fathers.
>
> My own father used to embarrass me by the way in which he looked at me. It was as if I were something too wonderful to be true, merely because I was there. I felt that if he were to utter what was in his heart, I would be covered with confusion at the vision of the marvel of my own existence. But of course he could not utter it. He simply looked at me, and at the other children, as if he were asking how he—inconsequential he—could be the father of beings so mysterious and marvelous.
>
> That was humility; but it was realism, too. Humility may be defined as right realism. And humility is necessary

for joy. A man will hardly appreciate a sunset if he imagines, in his pride, that he can paint something better.... And a father will not be happy in his children unless he realizes that they come from God, that they are held in existence from moment to moment by the power of God, and that but for God they would vanish in an instant into nothingness.

I wonder whether there can be a father so unappreciative as not to have felt, from time to time, a pang of unutterable happiness in his children....

There is a scene that I have seen several times; and to have seen it once would have repaid me immeasurably for every effort I have invested in fatherhood. It was the sight of a small boy, my son, and a small girl, my daughter, walking hand in hand into the twilight. Symphonies could be written about that. The greatest poets and dramatists could exhaust themselves attempting to express it in words. But it is unutterable....

I don't know what other fathers may feel, but I know what I feel at such moments. I feel that I am shouting together with all the sons of God....

This vision of the privilege of existence, and of the pricelessness of fatherhood, may come upon a man at any moment.[4]

Making It Happen—Have you experienced moments of "unutterable happiness" like those mentioned above? Preserve them in a journal...or on a sheet of paper placed into the family album. Your reflections will become special remembrances for you and your children in the years ahead—especially when they prepare to become parents themselves.

—

Daycare?

She watches over the affairs of her household
and does not eat the bread of idleness.
Her children arise and call her blessed;
her husband also, and he praises her:
"Many women do noble things,
but you surpass them all."
Charm is deceptive, and beauty is fleeting;
*but a woman who fears the L*ORD *is to be praised.*
Give her the reward she has earned,
and let her works bring her praise at the city gate.

(PROVERBS 31:27-31)

One hard decision many couples must make shortly after they find out they're expecting is whether mom will stay home and be a full-time mother or if she should return to the workplace. Often the decision is made on the basis of finances. Simply put, your family needs the money mom can make.

When our daughters were little, my wife, Beverly, stayed home. When the girls were school age, Bev went to work full-time—but she was blessed to be able to be the school secretary at the Christian school our girls attended. Steve's wife, Becky, was a full-time mom for 14 years. Then, as the boys got older, she began working part-time, still making sure she was home when school was out. When the boys became teenagers, she returned to work full-time.

If, for a season, mom must go back to work, can you two prayerfully plan a way for one of you to stay at home, perhaps working out of the home as a telecommuter or starting a home-based business?

Mom is indispensable at home; she cannot be replaced. Both of you are important in how your kids will develop. If you both must work, never let your jobs negatively impact your family life. *Never.* Get a different job, even if it means taking a pay cut, before you sacrifice your family to the pursuit of a higher standard of living.

Talk with your wife about the possibility of her being a full-time mom for a while. Although we live in a world that looks down on this at-home lifestyle, without question, it's the most fulfilling pattern for motherhood and wifehood your spouse can know.

Making It Happen—Sit down with your wife and make a list of pros and cons for mom going back to work versus staying home. Factor in the costs of daycare, wardrobe, gas, and other expenses entailed in working. If it's possible for your wife to work from home, do some brainstorming and see if you can come up with some good home-based businesses she can pursue—or even consider the possibility of her asking her employer if she can "telecommute" by doing her job at home.

Don't just take the easiest road. Weigh all the considerations, and pray for guidance. Your decision will make a huge impact on your child's life.

A New Perspective on Time

He has made everything beautiful in its time.

(ECCLESIASTES 3:11)

Not too long ago, when you were single, your time was your own. You came and went as you pleased. You ate when and what you wanted. If you felt like watching your favorite TV show, no one was there to distract you. If you wanted to stop by the gym for a workout on the way home from work, you did it.

And then the woman who is your child's mother came into your life, and soon things were different. You welcomed most of the new demands on your time because those were the hours in which your love grew.

Now there's an even newer demand on your time—and your wife's. You can no longer pick up and go as easily as before. Some activities you formerly enjoyed may have to be put off for some time.

But this new challenge to your Day-Timer is a *welcome* change. God has made everything beautiful in its time. And now is the time of fatherhood for you. A new season. A beautiful season.

So dad, embrace with full acceptance the necessary schedule adjustments that accompany fatherhood. In those hours you will find a reward far greater than those accorded by those activities you've left behind. And the day will come—far too soon—when the days of infancy are past, never to be regained.

You have only one season in which you can enjoy this child's infancy. Treasure this time. Treasure each season of fatherhood—they will not come to this child again. The time you have today will never come again. And though many fathers later regret the time they didn't spend with their growing children, I've yet to meet one who regrets spending too much time with his son or daughter.

That's especially true of new dads. You need some time to bond with this baby, and now is the best time of all because your wife can also use your presence around the house. Be there for both of them.

Making It Happen—Dad, how much vacation time do you have saved up at work? Does your company allow paternity leave? Can sick leave be used for new dads? Find out and arrange to take a few days off now while the baby is still young and mom needs you.

This time at home will not only facilitate bonding with the baby but will help you ease into your new role as you have more time to handle the baby, change diapers, and even bathe the baby. Now is a good time for a bit of a crash course in Dadhood 101.

A Lesson from Your Baby

Trust in the LORD with all your heart
and lean not on your own understanding;
in all your ways acknowledge him,
and he will make your paths straight.

(PROVERBS 3:5-6)

During the earliest stage of life, babies are completely dependent upon their parents to meet their every need. Babies cannot feed, change, bathe, or clothe themselves. When ill, children are totally in need of their parents' attention and remedies. They cannot provide for themselves a warm, safe, protected environment. They need help getting in or out of a crib, car seat, and playpen. They need to be shielded from harmful falls or objects, and if they move from room to room, they need to be carried around. Even the littlest things, such as wiping a runny nose or combing their hair, requires mom and dad's loving hands.

Have you ever thought about the fact that it's this very kind of dependence that God longs for in His children?

God promises and is faithful to feed and clothe us. He is our constant companion who is available to guide us in every circumstance of life, even the most difficult ones. The Bible describes Him as a Father who watches over us, cares for us, and protects us. He is the source of all we need.

Yet so often when it comes to the everyday matters of life, we forget to acknowledge our dependence upon Him. We even resist Him at times, like a disobedient toddler who wants to do the forbidden and is ignorant of the consequences.

Do you sometimes find yourself running your life your own way, in your own energy and wisdom? Do you incline toward an attitude of self-sufficiency, neglecting to include God in your decisions and doings?

In all that we do, the better way is to place ourselves completely in God's hands and "lean not on our own understanding" (Proverbs 3:5). That's what it means to trust Him with *all* your heart. And let's not limit our expressions of dependence upon Him to Sundays or just a few areas of our lives, but in all things, at all times. Let's make our dependence complete and invite God's participation at every moment in all that we do. Let's express the same dependence a baby does.

After all, God can do a better job of caring for us than we can...right?

Making It Happen—Dad, get into the habit of asking yourself, *Am I depending on God right now?* Ask this question all through the day—and notice the remarkable effect it can have on your perspective of what you are doing, and how.

Dedication—
More than a Ceremony

The LORD said to Moses,
"Consecrate to me every firstborn male.
The first offspring of every womb among the Israelites belongs to
me, whether man or animal."

(EXODUS 13:1-2)

Many churches celebrate the birth of a baby with a dedication ceremony. The parents bring their baby to the front of the church, the pastor dedicates the baby to God, and the mother and father also dedicate themselves as godly parents.

In liturgical churches, the infant is often baptized, a ritual that is meant to serve as a witness that the child belongs to God—though most denominations acknowledge the child must follow through with a personal commitment to Christ later, at some more mature age. The Roman Catholic faith practices christening as a similar affirmation of the parents' desire to raise the child as a Christian.

Often any of these three events, though meaningful, seem almost a given, a routine event that one simply *does.* But from God's point of view, when someone is dedicated to Him, it's serious business. God will take you up on your offer. He will do what you pray for. Dedication was, after all, His invention when He called for the firstborn of the Israelites to be offered to Him.

Today, under the New Testament, *all* we have is to be dedicated to God, not just a portion, not just the firstborn, not just the firstfruits of our labor.

Dad, as you and mom acknowledge God's ownership of your family, you're setting your child apart for God's use and yourselves apart to be God's representative parent here on earth.

But the dedication of a child isn't simply a one-time event that happens in front of the congregation at church. That act of dedication is lifelong—both your dedication to be the right dad for this child and the actual dedication of the child to God. Dedication is also an act of surrender, of saying to God, "Use this child, and use us, the parents, in any way that glorifies You." That may mean wonderful things, such as raising a child to be a great missionary, doctor, or intercessor. On the other hand, it might mean something entirely different, possibly even tragic in human terms. In life, sad things happen. Children get sick, they have accidents, they go astray, and some die young.

Of course, you don't want to even think about such possibilities. But if you can fully surrender this child, dedicating him or her to God without reservation, you'll find your years of fatherhood so much more rewarding. Nothing will faze you if you know without a doubt that this child belongs wholly to the Lord and has been entrusted to you by God.

As to your child's future: Let God be God. Give over that baby, *fully*. The result will be a miracle...no matter what happens.

Making It Happen—What is the tradition of your faith regarding newborn babies? Make plans with your pastor—and follow through. Take photos. When the baby is older and can understand, be sure and occasionally remind the child of this special day. Mark it on a calendar and celebrate it as a remembrance of that special day when this child was given to God.

Renewed Intimacy

*For this reason a man will leave his father and mother
and be united to his wife, and they will become one flesh.*

(Genesis 2:24)

It was good of God to invent sex, wasn't it? It's such an effective example of what the lives of a couple should be—one flesh. A man shall leave his father and mother and cleave to his wife and they shall be one flesh.

From this tremendous one-flesh experience comes a totally new individual—the fruit of a man and woman's deep love for one another. And this new person is part him, part her. What a fantastic plan! Who but God could come up with such a concept?

But often, in this sex-obsessed culture of ours, sex has become a trinket to be played with instead of the treasure God meant it to be. You will no doubt be hoping for renewed intimacy with your wife now that her pregnancy has concluded. But dad…a word to the wise: *Wait until she's ready.*

Mom's body has a lot going on right now. So do her emotions. She might be suffering from a slight depression. She might become impatient with you for no apparent reason as she must share your attention with the baby. Plus, some new moms may experience a slight fear of pregnancy again. This fear, however, is largely unjustified, especially if mom's nursing the baby. It's unlikely (but not impossible) she can conceive again for several months.

In time, things will settle down and your sex life will return to normal again. Until then, marvel at the plan of God to offer us this treasure of intimacy. Try to regard sex more as a treasure and never as a trinket. Steer clear of sexual temptations. They can destroy your life and your family.

Making It Happen—Dad, how's your thought life? Pure? Wavering? Light temptation? Heavy temptation? Men, unless we train our minds, unless we renew them as Paul encourages us in Romans 12:1-2, we're easy prey to lust—a sure short-circuit to healthy spiritual life, not to mention a means of robbing you and your wife of true intimacy.

Bring your thoughts under control. Learn to reject impure thoughts as soon as they arrive. These thoughts are no more than the "flaming arrows of the evil one," easily deflected by the shield of faith.

"...take up the shield of faith, with which you can extinguish all the flaming arrows of the evil one" (Ephesians 6:16-17).

Interacting with Your Baby

Be devoted to one another in brotherly love.

(ROMANS 12:10)

As a new father, you may be anxiously waiting for the day when your child is old enough to play ball, go fishing, join you on hikes, or play a game of checkers or chess. Obviously it's going to be a while before that can happen. But don't make the mistake of waiting until your child is older to begin interacting with him or her daily. While it's true that mom may be around the child more to nurture him or her (especially if the baby is still breast-feeding), and while moms are often viewed as the primary parent figure in an infant's life, we as dads need to make the most of every opportunity to bond with our child at as young an age as possible. The sooner you build those bonds, the stronger the relationship you'll have as your child grows up. Here are some suggestions for ways to interact with your child now and become an active and meaningful part of his or her life:

1. *Talk to your child.* Let him or her hear your voice, and speak in pleasant, happy tones. Say his or her name, and be encouraging. Though your baby cannot talk in response, he or she will communicate back to you through the eyes and the sounds and movements he or she makes. By talking, you'll lay the first stepping-stones toward making verbal interaction a natural part of both of your lives.

2. *Hold your child.* Babies thrive on hugs, being held, and affirming physical touch. As you work around the house, carry your child in a pack with you. When you go get the mail, bring him or her in your arms. Look for those opportunities to hold your little one for short or extended periods of time.

3. *Laugh with your child.* There's something about an adult's laugh that's contagious to a baby, and it often-times gets a baby to laugh, too. We've all heard that laughter is good medicine, and indeed it is. It's uplifting, fun, and encouraging, helping to give positive reinforcement to a child. Laughing along with your child will endear you to him or her.

4. *Change your child's diaper.* Before and after changing the diaper, you can play with your child's feet, gently tickle the tummy, let him or her grip your hand, and do small, gentle exercises of the limbs. You can talk or sing to your baby (don't worry if you can't sing on key—the little one won't notice).

By interacting with your infant, you'll get an early start on some of the most constructive bonding that can take place between you and your child. This, in turn, will become the foundation for a strong relationship that can last through the teen years and beyond.

Making It Happen—Each time you feed your baby or change his or her diaper, don't put him or her down immediately after you're done. Give at least four or five minutes of undivided attention to your baby, playing interactive games, talking, or playing with a toy.

Learning Fatherhood

Let us learn together what is good.

(JOB 34:4)

Men gravitate toward tasks they excel in. We recoil from chores that make us feel inept for fear of failure. Unfortunately in our culture, when it comes to being a good dad, many of us are apt to be the latter—feeling inept at the basics of fatherhood. The result is that some of us shy away from active fatherhood, preferring the safety of paternal passivity. After the initial excitement of their baby's birth, some well-meaning men return their energies to skills at which they're already comfortable—usually their career, a hobby, or financial advancement.

Perhaps that's where you are.

During the pregnancy, did you feel apprehensive about your ability to be a good father—even though you were excited about becoming a dad? And now that the baby is here and you're being called upon to do things that make you feel unskilled and uncomfortable, are you responding passively, avoiding such tasks as often as possible? If so, rest easy—you're not alone. Most of us need to learn how to be good fathers.

Sometimes learning fatherhood is like learning a foreign language or sailing on an unknown ocean without navigational tools. And yes, you may feel stretched out of your comfort zone at first. Although this is a natural reaction, it's easily remedied. Fatherhood isn't that hard to learn. Much of it is instinctive—if we prime the pump a bit and are willing to learn.

Do you remember when you first mastered a new skill? Maybe it was riding your first two-wheeler. Or holding a baseball bat over home plate. Or that promotion with a steep learning curve. Do you remember how *good* it felt as you slowly "got it"? The same thing will happen to you as a father. As you learn about fatherhood, you'll get better at it

Before long, you'll be delighted to find that some paternal instincts, perhaps buried by nonuse, will kick in—big time—and you'll find yourself a very fine father. Don't make the mistake many men do by giving up during the early days when your mistakes seem too many and your efforts too awkward and cumbersome. Someday your child will thank you for simply hanging in there. As for fearing failure, you're far more likely to fall short as a father if you remain passive.

Don't worry. You will indeed "get it"—if you remain teachable. And you'll receive the great joy common to fathers who have taken the time to master their "job specs" as dad—an appreciative and loving child. There is no greater reward.

Making It Happen—Set aside time each day to consult with dads who've gone before you by reading some of the many excellent books on Christian fatherhood (some of our favorites are listed in Appendix B at the end of this book). If you commute to work, listen to these books on audiotape. If you prefer to learn by watching, many excellent videos on fatherhood are available. Take a look at the great resources available from the National Fatherhood Initiative (www.fatherhood.org) or National Center for Fathering (www.fathers.com). Subscribe to the latter's magazine, *Today's Father* to get a regular update on good fathering tips.

Dads Do Diapers

He lifted me out of the slimy pit,
out of the mud and mire;
he set my feet on a rock
and gave me a firm place to stand.

(PSALM 40:2)

Okay, so the verse is taken a bit out of context…but dad, you too must sign up for diaper duty. Many will be the times when you'll lift Junior out of the slimy diaper, out of the mud and mire.

Only a generation ago, it was somewhat unusual for dads to do diaper duty. Some thoroughly macho men who could easily watch the blood flow at boxing matches somehow felt faint at the sight of a poopy diaper and enlisted mom to take charge. But in recent years, things have changed—for the better. Now many public men's restrooms offer changing tables where a dad can leap into action as Diaper Dad, the Mighty Warrior of the Cloth.

Sure, it's not a pleasant task, but once you get the hang of it, it's not so bad. And dad, this is just the beginning. Your young one will get into many a mess as he or she grows. Someday you may look back on your diaper days with fondness as your growing child finds new creative ways to make a mess of life.

Somehow God understands messes. Haven't you had a misstep or two recently that left somewhat of a stink, that needed a firm hand to clean up that which you were unable to remedy?

Like our children, we dads can mess up—big time. And God never fails to pick us up, clean up our mess, and reassure us that He still loves us and is our forgiving Father.

Making It Happen—Okay dad, roll up your sleeves and learn how to change diapers—and do so with the same tender care your heavenly Father exhibits when you've made a mess of things. If you're using disposable diapers, the simple directions are right on the package. Just read and do. (But be aware that one of the arguments against disposables is the combination of chemical and other artificial ingredients used in some diapers that will be in contact with your baby's skin.)

If you're using cloth diapers, changing can be a bit trickier. Appendix A on page 203 shows you how to fold a cloth diaper. If you choose cloth diapers, we strongly recommend using a diaper service, at least for the first few months—if you can find such a service. Many have gone out of business as most parents seem to prefer the convenience of disposables over the more traditional and environmentally sound cloth diapers. However, even if you prefer disposables, we still strongly recommend having a stash of cloth diapers handy. In addition to their obvious purpose, cloth diapers have a variety of other great uses:

- If you're away from home and need to change your baby and there's no comfortable surface for changing, place a cloth diaper or two under the infant.

—

- While in the car, if the sun is getting in your little one's eyes, tuck one edge of the cloth diaper into the top of the window and shut the window on it. This will make a nice shade from the sun.

- Little children often like to hold on to a soft blanket (like Linus in the "Peanuts" comic strip). A cloth diaper is great for this.

- Use a cloth diaper as a "burp cloth" for the times when you hold your baby against your shoulder to dislodge that elusive belch, often accompanied by a generous flow of "recycled" milk.

Even after your child no longer needs cloth diapers, you'll want to hang on to a small supply. They're great for wiping off the car, buffing your shoes, dusting furniture, and so on. In a nutshell, having cloth diapers handy will make your job as parents easier.

By the way, your newborn should be changed every two to three hours. Also watch for diaper rash. Treat it with over-the-counter creams for a couple of days, leave diapers off when possible, and if the rash persists, check with your doctor.

Handle with Care

The LORD watches over you—
the LORD is your shade at your right hand.

(PSALM 121:5)

I'll never forget how I felt when our first son became ill for the first time. Not only did he get sick, he became *very* sick. His temperature pushed 102 degrees (a rather dangerous level for an infant) and his normally energetic body was hot and listless. We immediately rushed him to the doctor for treatment, uncertain about what was wrong. Never have I felt a worse sense of helplessness than I did at that time. There's nothing more distressing to a parent than the possibility that an illness could endanger a baby's life. It pays to be prepared in advance with as much knowledge as possible when it comes to caring for your baby.

One of the most valuable investments you can make as parents is to buy one or two books on baby medical and health care. (In fact, my wife and I often give these as baby shower gifts. While such a gift is never as cute as a frilly little dress or a bib-style coverall, it's definitely a must-have for every home with a baby.) And it's *always* best to seek professional medical assistance from a doctor any time you have a question about your baby's health. You just don't want to take chances when it comes to your baby's safety.

Having said that, here are a few facts every parent should know:

Sudden Infant Death Syndrome (SIDS) is the most common cause of death in children up to one year old, striking one out of every 1000 babies. While experts still aren't sure what leads to it, they do advise the following:

1. Have your baby sleep on his or her back, not the front.

2. Use a firm mattress—no soft or cushy mattresses, pillows, blankets, or plush objects that might cause breathing problems for your baby.

3. Watch the room temperature (SIDS is more common in winter due to overheating).

4. Don't overdress your child to the point where he or she might become stuffy or hot.

For the latest and more detailed information, consult an up-to-date family medical book.

Fever or a high temperature is a common symptom when a baby is ill. Always call your doctor to see if a visit is recommended. If you're kept waiting, or if after a doctor's visit there's a relapse, you can cool your baby by putting him or her in a tub (preferably a baby tub) with an inch or two of lukewarm water and, using a washcloth or sponge, gently dabbing the water over his or her body. Consult with your doctor about whether any medication is advisable, and if he or she recommends a medicine that's available over the counter, be sure to have that medication on hand. (By the way, *never* leave a child alone during bath time. This is an absolute rule—even with the seemingly sturdy restraint devices designed for use in a tub. Leaving the bathroom for even a few seconds to answer the phone or do something else can prove fatal. If you have to leave, always take your baby with you.)

For safety's sake, always do a complete survey of your baby's surroundings. Is the mattress in the crib too small, leaving a space where he or she could get stuck? Do your crib, walker, and car seat all comply with current government safety codes? Are there any objects nearby that could stop your baby's breathing or choke him or her? Cultivate the habit of looking for potential hazards wherever you go. You'll be doing your child a great favor.

Making It Happen—Dad, if you don't already have one or two truly comprehensive baby medical guides on your shelf, go to a local bookstore as soon as possible. And if you already do, go ahead and buy an extra copy or two to give away at the next baby shower your wife attends.

One wise option is *The Baby Book: Everything You Need to Know About Your Baby from Birth to Age Two* by Dr. William and Martha Sears. This husband-and-wife author team has also written another fine book you'll want to have: *The Complete Book of Christian Parenting & Child Care: A Medical & Moral Guide to Raising Happy, Healthy Children.*

A Night Out

May your fountain be blessed,
and may you rejoice in the wife of your youth.

(PROVERBS 5:18)

If your situation is typical, a day or two after the baby's birth, both mom and infant come home from the hospital and life resumes—only now with a major adjustment, weighing about eight pounds. For several days, the adjustment is sweet—all that cooing from the crib and all the oohing and aahing from relatives and friends, not to mention from proud mama and papa.

But all too soon, mama is *tired*…as in *exhausted.* Dad, you too are feeling a bit overwhelmed by it all. That's okay. You're normal. And you need a break. You and your wife need a night out, a few choice hours to yourselves to get reacquainted with one another without that adorable distraction with the smelly diaper.

So my recommendation is that today you send your sweetheart some flowers with a note telling her of your love for her and asking her for a date this Saturday night. Arrange for a babysitter. No doubt grandma and grandpa will pitch in with gladness. They too need a little quality time alone with their new grandchild. But if they're not up to it or are unavailable, ask a trusted friend to pull baby-sitter duty Saturday. Make dinner reservations, get dressed up, and leisurely enjoy dinner at the finest restaurant you can afford. Relax. Enjoy one another. Remind each other why you married each other.

Don't stay out late, and keep your plans simple. Mom will get antsy anyway. Just make this a short break for her to get another view than that of the walls of your home. Also, watch for an appropriate time (probably over dinner) to remind your wife that you love her. Praise her for the mothering she's doing. Even if she seems to be having a hard time adjusting, find something to compliment her on.

End the evening with a simple present. A new pair of earrings, a card with a love coupon inside, or a gift certificate from her favorite store are all good choices. And don't expect the evening to lead to intimacy when you get home—that's not what this night is about.

And once you've really settled into parenthood, do this regularly. It doesn't always have to be dinner. Find creative ways to spend some time alone with your wife. Even a walk through the mall with a fast food dinner from the food court may be enough.

These breaks will rejuvenate you. And your baby will benefit from having a revitalized mom and dad.

Making It Happen—A checklist for your big night:

1. Call the florist.
2. Ask your wife if Saturday is a good night to slip away. If not, how about Sunday night?
3. Make dinner reservations.
4. Call the grandparents or some other trusted sitter.
5. Choose a mushy greeting card to give your wife at dinner.
6. Pick out a simple gift to give her at the close of dinner.
7. *Rejoice in the wife of your youth.*

Our Heavenly Helper

Those who hope in the LORD
will renew their strength.
They will soar on wings like eagles;
they will run and not grow weary,
they will walk and not be faint.

(ISAIAH 40:31)

As a father, you'll definitely have days when you just can't seem to keep up with all the demands of being a dad. You'll wish you had extra hands, extra time, extra stamina, or even extra patience. When it comes to raising a baby, you pretty much have to stay on your toes all the time—always alert to whatever your baby might need, always ready for that next "crisis."

When you consider the enormous responsibilities of parenthood, you can see why God's original design for the family makes such great sense. Beginning with Adam and Eve, God affirmed His intent for a husband and wife to work together as a team in raising up a family. Both a father and a mother each have unique contributions they can make to the growth of their children, and together, they can accomplish a task that's much more daunting for just one person alone.

Yet even as a couple, you'll have times when you feel overwhelmed and wonder how you're going to make it to the next day. That's good, because it's easy for us to forget that we have a third helper available to us—God Himself!

Have you invited God to help you carry out your work as parents? Do you deliberately ask for His wisdom when you make decisions, His strength when you're tired, His peace when you're concerned? Do you ask Him for patience when you're at the brink of frustration, or joy when you're facing discouragement?

God knows exactly how it feels to be a parent. All through the Old Testament, we see God as a parent caring for the children of Israel. And it wasn't an easy task. Time and again, the Israelites stubbornly rebelled against God, yet He still fulfilled His promises to protect them and provide for them. In Exodus 34:6-7 (NKJV) we read that God, in His care for His people, is "merciful and gracious, longsuffering, and abounding in goodness and truth, keeping mercy for thousands, forgiving iniquity and transgression and sin." That same care extends to those of us who have received Christ as our Savior, for according to John 1:12, we are "children of God." And all of us can probably think of times when we, like the Israelites, have made God's job as a parent a bit difficult!

Yes, God knows the challenges of parenthood. And because He has infinite wisdom, infinite patience, and infinite strength, He is more than able to rise to those challenges. Are you and your spouse inviting Him to join you in the task of parenting? Are you bringing your specific requests to Him? You'll find that including God in all that you do as parents definitely makes the work more manageable and more fulfilling.

Making It Happen—What are your needs right now as parents? Write four or five of your greatest needs on a sheet of paper and put it in a prominent place. Each time you look at the list, lift up your needs in prayer. Then watch carefully and see how God answers. Sometimes He may do so in subtle ways. When you notice answers to your prayers, offer God a prayer of thanks.

—

Overcoming a Poor Role Model

I will give you a new heart
and put a new spirit in you;
I will remove from you your heart of stone
and give you a heart of flesh.

(Ezekiel 36:26)

Many new dads face a huge obstacle as they enter fatherhood: Their own father wasn't a very good role model. Many men from the generation now becoming fathers were raised in homes where dad was gone or disinterested. If that's true in your case, you remember the many nights you hurt inside because dad wasn't there for you—even if he lived in the same house.

So what do you do now that *you're* the dad? Repeat the cycle, inflicting that identical wound on your own child?

If you remember the intensity of that pain, there's no way you'll pass it on to that new baby—even if you sometimes feel like splitting.

Instead, here's what you do: If there's bitterness toward your father, ask God, by His Spirit, to give you a new heart toward your father...and certainly toward your new baby.

Realize that *God is the ultimate good Father.* He not only can redeem the damage done in your own life by your very imperfect father, He can take up the slack where you fail as a father. But if you really come to know Him as your Father, you'll find yourself failing less and less as a dad.

—

Making It Happen—If you've never done so before and need to do so, forgive your father for his mistakes, for his meanness, for all the times he wasn't there for you. If you can't think of anything you need to forgive your dad for, call him and thank him for modeling fatherhood for you. If you can't call, pick out a nice card and send it with a note of thanks.

To Pacify or Not to Pacify

Naomi took the child and laid him on her bosom,
and became a nurse to him.

(Ruth 4:16 nkjv)

As a new parent, you'll quickly discover that certain issues seem to spark passionate debates everywhere you go. Cloth diapers or disposable diapers? Breast-feeding or bottle-feeding? Pacifiers or no pacifiers? Let's consider that last one.

For starters, babies seem to have a compelling need to suck on something *apart* from when they're feeding. You may have noticed this. For example, if you bring a finger close to your baby's mouth, you may find him or her wanting to suck it. Or, you may have seen him or her suck on their own fingers. And there's no question that this action of sucking seems to calm or pacify a baby (hence the term "pacifier"). In fact, it's common for babies to fall asleep while sucking on a pacifier.

But one of the arguments against pacifiers (and finger sucking) is their potential to damage teeth or affect the mouth in some way. Another concern is that harmful germs on a baby's hands can end up being introduced into the body through the mouth. There's also the chance that a parent might attempt to use a pacifier to soothe a baby when the baby is hollering because of a specific problem—and the parent will fail to notice that problem because he's so preoccupied with trying to calm the baby with a pacifier.

While medical and dental experts land on both sides of this issue, based on the books and websites we've consulted, there does seem to be a general agreement that pacifier use during the first couple of years isn't harmful on the teeth. From about age two onward, however, pacifier use can become detrimental.

In addition, a pacifier can give a mother's sore nipples some much-needed relief. And, if you're trying to lull your little one to sleep, a pacifier will usually do the trick.

If you do decide to use a pacifier, make sure it includes of these features:

- The nipple is one piece of material and is specifically intended for mouth use.

- The shield is not removable and has holes for saliva flow.

- The nipple is without tears or holes or loose pieces that can harbor dangerous bacteria or break loose in baby's mouth.

- The pacifier is frequently sterilized in boiling water.

- The pacifier is never tied to a string or neck-piece that could strangle your baby.

- If your baby is chewing on the pacifier, it's time to replace it with a teething ring.

Making It Happen—Talk with your spouse about the pros and cons of using a pacifier, and make a decision together. Check several parenting books and websites and weigh the various factors yourself. And finally, as your baby gets older, make a gradual and deliberate attempt to wean him or her from pacifier use.

Making Music

Speak to one another with psalms,
hymns and spiritual songs.
Sing and make music in your heart to the Lord,
always giving thanks to God the Father for everything,
in the name of our Lord Jesus Christ.

(Ephesians 5:19-20)

Some of a child's earliest memories will be of the songs he or she heard over and over again, whether in nursery rhyme form ("Three Blind Mice"), at the church nursery ("Jesus Loves Me"), or from mom and dad. In the latter case, shortly after each of my girls was born, I selected a song just for them and sang it to them each night as I tucked them in. They were very young when I began this ritual and probably don't remember the earliest occasions of hearing dad's horribly monotone voice singing them to sleep...but as the practice continued, it built some wonderful memories. At my middle daughter's wedding, she surprised me by playing a tape of "our song" and asking me to dance with her in front of the guests. The song was "Side by Side," and neither Rebecca nor I can hear that song without wonderful memories.

For Rachel, our song was "Love Me Tender," although I don't sound a bit like Elvis. And for Bethany, our song was "You Are My Sunshine." Each song is truly *our* song, and I heartily recommend this version of "making melody."

Dad, not only is this a great memory maker, but studies show several positive results when a young infant is exposed to music. Accordingly, many hospital nurseries play tapes of lullabies to soothe the babies in their care.

Making It Happen—Make sure your baby's nursery is musically equipped with a CD player, a radio, or even a small music box that plays a simple tune. But in addition to these electronic music makers, you can make your own music.

Here are some ideas on providing music for your child:

1. Sing to your child occasionally—even if your voice is, like mine, a complete monotone. To your child, your voice is like music from heaven. And dads, here's where you can really shine. The low, soft tones of your voice are particularly appealing to babies.

2. Provide an occasional nighttime treat of soft, relaxing music—lullabies—to your child as he or she sleeps.

3. Choose a few age-appropriate musical wind up toys. But never force music on your baby, and if tears consistently flow when the music begins, try another style, or stop the music until a later day, and then try again.

4. The first songs many children learn are actually rich in solid Christian teaching. There's not a better lesson for a child to learn than the endearing words:

> Jesus loves me, this I know,
> For the Bible tells me so.
> Little ones to Him belong.
> They are weak but He is strong.

5. Finally dad, don't raise your baby on the junk food of loud ear-pounding music. Not only is it hard on their young ears, but it can make them more irritable and jittery. They will hear plenty of that kind of music throughout life without your help. Your job is to provide music that, like David's harp, soothes the baby's soul.

Dad, one of your child's fondest memories will be of your voice and your laughter. Don't deprive your baby of this treasure.

No Two Children Are Alike

*My frame was not hidden from you
when I was made in the secret place.*

(PSALM 139:15)

Ever notice a peculiar phenomenon that occurs whenever young mothers get together and one of them happens to be pregnant?

Without fail, the moms will immediately begin to compare notes about their pregnancy experiences. They'll say, "Every morning I felt so sick...at midnight I would have a craving for pickles and ice cream...I was so thrilled when I felt the first kick...I was in labor this many hours...."

This same phenomenon is even more marked when it comes to babies. Wherever new moms and dads gather, you can be sure they'll talk about their babies' first sounds, first movements, first laugh, first steps, first words, first everything. They'll tell you the month, day, hour, and minute their little one first pointed to the dog and said, "Kitty?" Then they'll ask, "Has your baby said kitty yet?"

Well, maybe it's not *that* bad. But the point is, when other parents share (or should we call it subtle bragging?) about how quickly their child has reached certain milestones, sometimes we can't help but worry a little if our same-age child doesn't seem to be approaching that milestone yet.

For example, our first son, Keith, was a late bloomer when it came to walking. While other little ones were becoming quite skilled at fleeing from their parents' grasp, Keith was perfectly content to continue crawling. Every time we encouraged him to walk, he would slowly tumble right back down to the floor.

Because Keith was in the top 95 percentile in height and weight for his age, we began to speculate that perhaps his height and weight were out of proportion to the development of the coordination skills he needed for walking. We posed the question to a pediatrician, who suggested we get thick-soled, high-top shoes almost resembling hiking boots. These offered the support Keith needed, and sure enough, he began to take up the challenge of learning to walk.

I say all this to make a simple point: All babies develop at different rates. When we hear about so-and-so's baby doing such-and-such by a certain age, we should avoid using that as a standard for our own child's development. Give your baby time; he or she might simply be a late bloomer. And if you feel there's reason to be concerned, check with your pediatrician, who will be able to tell you the approximate time spans in which you can expect certain developments to take place.

Your child is a unique creation. Rejoice in that, and celebrate each new accomplishment as it comes. And rejoice as well with other parents in the accomplishments of their little ones. That makes the joy of parenting much richer for everyone.

Making It Happen—If you would like a good book that explains the developmental progress of a child during the first 12 months, you may want to purchase *The Joy of Fatherhood* by Marcus Jacob Goldman, M.D. (Roseville, CA: Prima Publishing, 2000).

Your Compass for All of Life

Your word is a lamp to my feet
and a light for my path.

(PSALM 119:105)

Have you ever attempted to find constellations in the night sky? Perhaps for fun, you've done a bit of amateur astronomy and have been able to locate certain stars, planets, or even distant galaxies such as Andromeda. Or, maybe you've simply enjoyed marveling at the immensity of our universe. Whatever the case, chances are that your interest in the evening sky has been a matter of pleasure rather than necessity.

But for sailors of centuries past, the study of the stars was a matter of life and death. A ship's navigator depended on the stellar bodies to help him determine the ship's location and plot the next day's journey. Foggy or cloudy nights made it impossible to chart the course and often caused miscalculations that led to a crew's demise.

The same is true for us today as Christians. We live in a world that's hopelessly adrift in the darkness of sin. What's our point of reference for charting the right course? God's Word, the Bible. When we look to Scripture for guidance, we will know the direction the Lord desires for us to take in all that we do. It's the light of God's Word that helps us guide the ship of our life to the desired destination.

How well acquainted are you with your point of reference? Are you taking time—even if it's just two or three minutes a day—to check your bearings and to get to know God Himself better? As a new dad, your familiarity with God's Word becomes more important than ever. For as your child grows up, he or she will watch you chart the path of your life. As a father, you have the opportunity to pass some vital "navigation skills" to the next generation.

No, you don't need to become a Bible scholar. But the Bible does encourage us to "let the word of Christ dwell in you richly" (Colossians 3:16). We're exhorted to soak in God's Word in the same way that a sponge soaks up water.

Psalm 1:3 paints a beautiful picture of what happens to the person who delights in God's Word: "He is like a tree planted by streams of water, which yields its fruit in season and whose leaf does not wither. Whatever he does prospers." Do you want to know that kind of fruitfulness in your life? Then soak in God's Word and let it guide your steps. When it comes to navigating the direction you take in life, a compass is a necessity—and there's no better compass than God's Word.

Making It Happen—Do you spend time in God's Word? And more importantly, do you set aside that time not because you *have* to, but because you *want* to? What are some ways you can soak up more of God's Word in your life?

One way you can grow more in the Bible is to record a book of the Bible in your own voice —perhaps the book of John—to play back to yourself while commuting or on trips.

The Greatest Investment of All

Sons are a heritage from the LORD,
children a reward from him.

(PSALM 127:3)

When it comes to financial investments, we like to see a return on our money. Before we place our hard-earned dollars into a stock, mutual fund, money-market account, or any other investment vehicle, we will often do comparison shopping to see which option will get the best return. It doesn't make sense to invest in such a way that we end up with less money rather than more.

But there's one investment you cannot evaluate on the basis of monetary return. It's an investment that requires a significant amount of money, and you can't expect any of it to be returned—ever. That may not sound like a wise investment, but it's one of the best ones of all.

What is this investment? Raising a child. According to the Expenditures on Children by Families 2000 Annual Report, the cost of raising a child to age 18 is now $165,630. If you already have more than one child, you can probably testify that your monthly income definitely doesn't go as far as it used to! Yet when it comes to children, you can't measure the return in terms of dollars.

What is it that we as fathers *do* get in return?

- the most angelic facial expressions while your little one is asleep

- an admirer who thinks you know everything (at least till the teen years!)

- an enthusiastic hug at the door, no matter how many things you did wrong at work that day

- a wonderful curiosity about the mysteries of life—what makes a heart beat, the size of outer space, the source of lightning and thunder

- a carefree enthusiasm for the simpler things in life—balloons, pets, a sprinkler on a hot day, ice cream

- a constant reminder of how amazing God's creation is

- the best artwork that ever hung on a refrigerator

- a good excuse to read all your favorite children's books again and watch those silly cartoon reruns

- the inner joy that wells up inside when your child gets that first base hit, performs that first recital, does a solo in the school program

- handmade, one-of-a-kind gifts and cards for Christmas, Father's Day, or "just 'cuz I love you, Daddy."

Raising a child yields returns that cannot be measured financially. In fact, what children give to their dads and moms each day is truly priceless. The joy they give cannot be found on any store shelf, cannot be bought with any amount of money.

Yes, parents are the richest people in the world.

Making It Happen—Write a list of some of the "returns" you've received from your little one. Share this list with your wife, and see if you can come up with more "returns" together. Save this list in an appropriate place, such as a baby scrapbook or a photo album. Years from now, this list will bring back happy memories of your first years as parents.

The Visible God

For you know that we dealt with each of you
as a father deals with his own children,
encouraging, comforting and urging you
to live lives worthy of God,
who calls you into his kingdom and glory.

(1 Thessalonians 2:11-13)

How will your children come to know the Lord? How can they ever *see* the invisible God? Simple: God has designed fatherhood as a means for men to display the attributes of God to their children. Dad, you're the visible presence of the invisible God. When your hands are holding your baby, those hands become, in a real sense, God's hands. Your strong arms of protection represent God's strong protection. Your body is the temple of God, and as you are submitted to Him as Lord, your work on this earth is His work through you. This is especially so with your role as a father.

Most of us have heard that a child's perception of God is largely a reflection of his perception of his earthly father. A harsh, demanding father at home will likely raise a child with a distorted image of an unloving, dictatorial God. A loving father who understands that he acts as an earthly proxy for our heavenly Father will demonstrate the love of God to the child, resulting in a spiritually perceptive and healthy child, and later, adult.

Dad, it's an awesome and wonderful responsibility you bear. Walk gently. Be to your child all that your heavenly Father is to you.

Making It Happen—Make a list of at least a dozen different attributes of God. Think of ways to incorporate these character qualities into your own life. You may want to make a photocopy of this page and tape it someplace prominent where you can remind yourself of the fatherly qualities you're cultivating.

1.

2.

3.

4.

5.

6.

7.

8.

9.

10.

11.

12.

Baby by the Book

*Only be careful, and watch yourselves closely
so that you do not forget the things your eyes have seen
or let them slip from your heart as long as you live.
Teach them to your children and to their children after them.*

(DEUTERONOMY 4:9)

Dad, start your child with books right away. Your first purchases can be simple "board books" that teach a child colors, numbers, letters, and common words. Even a very small infant will respond favorably to a father's voice as he reads aloud. Some expectant parents have even read to the baby while still in the womb.

Over time, these little ones who have been exposed to stories, words, and the voices of their parents will turn into toddlers who will make frequent trips to daddy's lap carrying his or her favorite book.

And of course, include Bible stories in your early reading. You might even try your hand at retelling some favorite stories in your own words: Daniel in the lion's den, David and Goliath, Ruth and Naomi, Abraham and Isaac, the Prodigal Son, and other parables of Jesus make fine stories. And at Christmas and Easter, include the retelling of the Lord's lowly birth in the stable and the Lord's death, burial, and resurrection. It doesn't matter how young the audience—these stories are being implanted in the child's heart and mind.

You will give your children a great source of wealth by instilling in them a joy of stories at an early age. And don't be surprised at how much fun you'll get out the stories, too. Even on the ninety-seventh time you've heard each one!

Making It Happen—Some good titles to start your little one's library include:

The New Bible in Pictures for Little Eyes by Kenneth N. Taylor

Goodnight Moon by Margaret Wise Brown

Aesop's Fables

Pat the Bunny by Dorothy Kunhardt

Don't forget to include the books you loved as child. Can you remember a couple of titles? Chances are, if you loved them, they were probably popular with other children and are still in print.

Laughter, the Sign
of a Happy Home

A cheerful heart is good medicine.

(PROVERBS 17:22)

Laughter is an essential part of fatherhood. It brings good cheer into the home, helping to relieve stress and provide a much-needed balance to the heaviness of life's responsibilities. When you're able to smile and laugh, you nurture a healthy atmosphere that makes for a happier wife and lighthearted children. Proverbs 15:13 tells us, "A happy heart makes the face cheerful."

As a dad, you'll find plenty of reasons to laugh. Your children, through their actions and words, will bring many a smile to your face. Even in their mistakes and misbehavior, your kids will do funny things that will make it hard for you to hide your smile behind a straight face.

For example, when our youngest son, Ryan, was three years old, somehow he got hold of a pair of scissors and my favorite dress sweater and zealously snipped away till the sweater looked as if it had been run through a paper shredder. The crime was serious enough that it merited an appropriate punishment, but at the same time, his diligent handiwork had so thoroughly decimated the sweater that we couldn't help but laugh (and yes, I still have the sweater, which brings a smile to me whenever I look at it).

As children grow older, they come to love jokes and opportunities to laugh. Don't discourage this; use it to help your children develop a good sense of humor. Teach your children the difference between good-natured and positive joking, and jokes that demean or hurt others. And be willing to let your children aim their good-humored laughs at you, too! For some reason, kids find it hard to resist teasing their parents, and when it's done right, they'll enjoy having you laugh along with them.

Do you find it easy to smile and laugh now? If not, think about others around you whom you can learn from. Resolve to not take life too seriously all the time, and to do what you can to bring cheerfulness to your home. And if laughter isn't a problem for you, then you can be sure your kids will find it contagious. Children love a happy home—and you, as a dad, are a big part of making that happy home possible.

Making It Happen—What is the "cheerfulness level" of your home now? Are you making any effort to contribute to it? What about at the workplace? And are you careful to use your humor in ways that don't leave negative impressions or dishonor God? What can you do as a dad to contribute to a happier atmosphere in your home? Think of two or three specific answers you can apply, beginning today.

The Future Is in Your Hands

"For I know the plans I have for you," declares the LORD,
*"plans to prosper you and not to harm you, plans to give
you hope and a future. Then you will call upon me and come
and pray to me, and I will listen to you. You will seek me and
find me when you seek me with all your heart."*

(JEREMIAH 29:11-13)

Have you had the experience yet of holding your baby in your arms and projecting ahead, trying to see your child's future? It's awesome. What's now a small bundle of blankets and gurgles will eventually morph into a man or woman with a life of joys and sadnesses, triumphs and tragedies. Some of what will happen will depend on you. Through your prayers and your faithfulness to be there for your child, you will play a significant—even *determining*—role in the outcome of your child's future.

God has a plan for your child. And you're one of the primary vehicles through which He wishes to put that plan into action. For the first two decades of life (at least) you will be the shaper, former, and data-inputer that will influence the fate of this human being.

If you ever leave him or her, fail to provide, or cut off communication by putting your own needs and desires ahead of your child's, you will very likely have ensured a hard future for this, your most precious progeny.

But if you see in your small baby the hopes and dreams he or she will someday have—if you see what God sees—you'll nourish that child to a successful adult life. And that, Dad, will be its own reward.

Making It Happen—Look around you at some of the people you know who have been abandoned or ignored by their dads. Maybe you need look no farther than the mirror.

If you ask anyone who was raised with an absent father (either physically or emotionally), they will likely tell you how tough it *still* is to work through that leaky childhood.

Your role is critical to your child's future.

Never forget that.

Never leave your child the inheritance of abandonment.

God Is with You

Do not let this Book of the Law depart from your mouth;
meditate on it day and night....Then you will be
prosperous and successful....Be strong and courageous.
Do not be terrified; do not be discouraged, for the LORD
your God will be with you wherever you go.

(JOSHUA 1:8-9)

When Moses died, Joshua had big shoes to fill. Not only was he to become the new leader of the nation of Israel, he was also to take the Israelites into the Promised Land and initiate a massive conquest of the land by overtaking the seemingly unconquerable city of Jericho. Joshua may have felt nervous and uncertain of himself, for the Lord took the time to come alongside him with the encouragement in Joshua 1:8-9.

As a dad, you are a leader, too. You're called to lead your family in the face of whatever challenges the world might offer. And like Joshua, you can take comfort in the promises God offers to one who looks to His Word for guidance. Let's look at God's promises to Joshua and see how they might apply to us today as we abide in Him and His Word.

God promises success. In John 15:5 (NKJV), Jesus said, "I am the vine, you are the branches. He who abides in Me, and I in him, bears much fruit; for without Me you can do nothing." Our fruitfulness in life—our success—is wholly dependent upon living as a branch that abides in the vine. Apart from the vine, Jesus Christ, we cannot bear fruit. The success God promises can be manifest in many ways, not just physical prosperity. God's kind of success is different from what we often label as success, but it's a much better kind.

God promises His presence. God told Joshua, "I will be with you wherever you go." And the Lord gives that same promise to us today: "Never will I leave you; never will I forsake you" (Hebrews 13:5). Note what the very next verse says, "So we say with confidence, 'The Lord is my helper; I will not be afraid' " (verse 6). Because God promises to stay with us, we have nothing to fear. We can "be strong and courageous," as Joshua 1:9 says.

When it comes to leading your family, the challenges before you may be great, just as they were for Joshua. But when we as dads abide in the Lord, we will know success. Through our connection with the vine, we will bear fruit. And we can always count on God's presence, no matter what. We're not in this battle alone; we have God Himself at our side. You'll find these promises a tremendous source of confidence in your leadership as a dad!

Making It Happen—Are there any challenges facing you right now that have you feeling fearful or dismayed? Write them here, and be specific. Then pray about them, yielding your concerns to the Lord, and rest in His promises to stand with you and bless you as you abide in Him.

The Lesson of the Rats

Honor one another above yourselves.

(ROMANS 12:10)

One of the more valuable parenting lessons I learned came not from a pastor, a counselor, a grandparent, a family member, or a parenting book or magazine. Those are all great sources for parenting advice, but in this particular case, the lesson came from a rather unusual source. Two groups of white laboratory rats, to be exact.

I learned about the story of the rats in one of my college classes. It turns out there was a psychology course in which a professor told one group of students, "I'm going to give you some white rats to care for. These rats are exceptionally bright. They do very well in mazes and on other tests. You'll enjoy working with them." Then to another group of students he said, "You'll be responsible for testing and caring for some rats that aren't very bright. They have done poorly in mazes and other tests. You'll find them generally stubborn and unresponsive."

Now, the students with the bright rats treated them well, played with them, and lavished them with attention. As promised, these rats performed superbly. But the students who had been given the not-so-smart rats didn't give them any special treatment. In fact, they handled the rats roughly. And, as expected, the rats didn't perform well.

What the students didn't know is that *all* the rats were equally bright. So why the difference in the way the two groups performed? It all came down to the students' expectations of the rats and how they treated them.

That principle applies to parent-baby relationships as well. Though a baby can't comprehend our words, the tone of our voice and the manner in which we touch reveals whether we are happy or angry, patient or frustrated, caring or uncaring. And that, in turn, affects our little one's responses to us.

Many times when I caught myself being impatient with Keith, Nathan, or Ryan, or possibly making wrong assumptions about them, the lesson of the rats would suddenly come to mind. I'd be reminded that, like the second group of students, I might not be "reading" the situation right. I'd remember that special treatment really does make a difference—a big difference.

And when it comes to babies, we're not talking about mere rats. We're talking about a gift from God Himself. Such a gift is well worthy of special treatment...don't you agree?

Making It Happen—What are two or three ways you can visibly demonstrate special treatment to your baby every day? Put one of these into action today, and commit yourself to showing special attention to your child on an ongoing basis.

What Is Father-Love?

For if, when we were God's enemies,
we were reconciled to him through the death
of his Son, how much more, having been reconciled,
shall we be saved through his life!

(ROMANS 5:10)

Nowhere is the depth of a father's love demonstrated more clearly than in God's love toward us, His children. This love is so profound, so past understanding, that God chose to demonstrate love to not only His obedient children but to His *dis*obedient kids as well—His enemies.

In a word, God's Father-love toward us was and is and always will be *sacrificial.* Christ's death on the cross was, after all, a sacrifice for us—a *supreme* sacrifice. In our society, the idea of love seems to have more to do with warm fuzzy emotional feelings than with sacrifice. Especially *willing* sacrifice.

When that new baby of yours was born into this world, he or she was given as God's opportunity for you to learn to sacrifice. At times you'll be called on to joyfully give up your physical comfort (can anyone say 3:00 A.M. feedings or unpleasant diaper changes?), your financial "wants" (sorry, dad, you may have to postpone that new fishing rod, car, or vacation), your free time (would you really enjoy the football game knowing you were missing your daughter's piano recital?). But what do you suppose is the reward for the sacrifices of love?

The answer in a word: *joy.* It was "for the joy set before him" that Jesus "endured the cross" (Hebrews 12:2). And as we learn

to demonstrate our father-love through sacrifice, we will experience a unique and powerful sense of joy that God ensures can
come from no other source on earth.

Making It Happen—Start practicing sacrificial
living today by finding a way to do something for
your wife that will ease her load. Fix dinner?
Clean the house? Do the laundry? Give her a
lengthy backrub? Doing all of the above will earn
you some big points toward Husband of the
Year.

You Were Chosen

For we are God's workmanship,
created in Christ Jesus to do good works,
which God prepared in advance for us to do.

(EPHESIANS 2:10)

Has it occurred to you yet that the new resident at your address didn't show up by accident? It wasn't simply a biological process that brought that baby into your life—though it was through biology (and perhaps adoption) that God accomplished His goal of giving you the baby He had in mind.

You've been chosen by God for an incredibly important job. You were handpicked to be the father of *this* child—for as long as you or the child shall live. In choosing you, God also equipped you. You have everything you need to be the *exact* father that child needs. However, you must be faithful. You must *know* that you've been called to fatherhood as surely as a missionary is called to foreign lands. For in a sense, this child *is* a mission field—and you're the missionary. You've been elected to serve, to feed, to teach this little one.

You're the one for this child. *The only one.*

Making It Happen—How about taking a moment to offer a prayer of thanks to God for choosing you to be this child's father?

Lord, I thank You for the unspeakable privilege of being this child's father. I'm honored that You have sent this child specifically for me to tend and nurture. May I be faithful to reflect that honor. Show me, God, when I'm on the wrong track. Help me see the special needs—and the talents—this child has.

Lord, when this child is grown, may there be few regrets at the way I've performed the task You've given me.

Thank You, Lord. Thank You!

Stretching the Money

Which of you, if his son asks for bread,
will give him a stone?
Or if he asks for a fish, will give him a snake?
If you, then, though you are evil,
know how to give good gifts to your children,
how much more will your Father in heaven
give good gifts to those who ask him!

(MATTHEW 7:9-12)

Many couples postpone having children until they think they can afford a child. But in so doing, they miss many blessings from God. A baby is a *gift,* and delaying the reception of God's gifts until you feel financially secure may mean a very long wait. Even then, a Christian must still live by faith, depending on God and not on his own ability to create wealth. When it comes to parenthood, the old saying "where God guides, God provides" can be amended to "when God gives the blessing of a baby, He gives the means to take care of that baby."

Perhaps money is tight for you right now. Maybe this baby, though loved by you, is proving to be an unexpected challenge to the budget. You may disagree with your wife about money matters—a common problem in young marriages. Don't let it be one in yours.

By an act of your will, *determine to trust God for your finances.* That's of course the way it should be with any Christian man or woman—a life of trusting God for His provision. But the arrival of a baby often serves as a reminder of just how much we need to depend on Him for everything.

To ease your concerns about finances, you'll need to do two things.

First, make a commitment to trust in God, laying all your financial considerations before your heavenly Father. Look to Him as your source. Know that He will provide.

Second, learn the basic principles of money management as taught in the Bible. Yes, God has much to say to dads about how to prosper, and most of it is not the advice many young men are following.

Making It Happen—I suggest you and your wife read together *The Complete Financial Guide for Young Couples: A Lifetime Approach to Spending, Saving and Investing* by Larry Burkett. Larry is perhaps the best-known Christian financial counselor writing today. Here's just one example of the wisdom you can glean from his book:

> The average young married couple tries to accumulate in about three years what it should take thirty years to accumulate. Consequently, what they do accumulate is an enormous amount of debt. As a result of debt, they have financial pressures; as a result of financial pressures, they stop communicating. They cease to be companions and, instead, they become combatants.[5]

Larry Burkett's very informative website is found at www.crown.org. Check it out.

Dad, know that God wants you to provide well for your family—by looking to Him.

Learn to be a faithful dad in money matters.

—

A Father's Trust in God

Abraham looked up and there in a thicket
he saw a ram caught by its horns. He went over and
took the ram and sacrificed it as a burnt offering instead of his
son. So Abraham called that place The LORD Will Provide.
And to this day it is said, "On the mountain
of the LORD it will be provided."

(GENESIS 22:13-14)

The story of Abraham and Isaac has to be one of the most heart-wrenching father-child stories in the Bible. God had promised Abraham and Sarah a son many years earlier. Finally, after Abraham's fiasco with his wife's handmaiden, Hagar, which produced a son, Ishmael, God does indeed provide the promised son through Sarah.

What a blessing! The child of promise. Abraham was over-joyed—and so was Sarah. Joy was the order of the day for Mr. and Mrs. Abraham.

Fast-forward a few years. God says to Abraham, "Take your son, your only son Isaac, whom you love, and go to the region of Moriah. Sacrifice him there as a burnt offering on one of the mountains I will tell you about" (Genesis 22:2).

Huh? Do *what*, Lord?

Put yourself in Abraham's shoes. Imagine the turmoil he must have gone through! And yet that turmoil isn't recorded in Scripture—only that Abraham did what God said. And on the mountain, when Isaac asked where the lamb was for the offer-ing, Abraham, still trusting God, replied, "God Himself will provide the lamb for the burnt offering, my son" (verse 8).

Abraham then bound Isaac on the altar and "reached out his hand and took the knife to slay his son." It was at that point that God called out to Abraham, "Do not lay a hand on the boy....Now I know that you fear God, because you have not withheld from me your son, your only son" (verses 10-12).

God then did indeed supply the sacrifice—a ram caught in the thicket by its horns. The story concludes with God promising to bless Abraham and his descendents because of his faith and obedience in surrendering that which was most precious to him—his child.

Dad, this story depicts so clearly the ultimate trust a father must have—willingly surrendering a child for the purposes of God. It takes a man of faith to say, "Take this child, Father, for whatever purposes You deem right. I surrender this child to You—entirely."

Making It Happen—Today, let that be your prayer. It may be hard to come to that place of total surrender, but once the child is offered on the altar for God, the blessing will come in God's way. Trust Him, dad. Trust Him.

Spiritual Immunization

Be…innocent about what is evil.

(Romans 16:19)

When it comes to immunization, who do you think experiences more pain—the baby, who doesn't understand why he or she is being pricked with a sharp needle, or the parents, whose hearts bleed with compassion and who would gladly take the shots for baby if they could?

Though we may feel terrible about subjecting a baby to painful immunization shots, we know there's really no other alternative for protecting our baby's health from destructive or life-threatening illnesses. Just one serious illness is all it takes to leave lifelong scars of one kind or another on your child's body.

What's more, as Christian parents, physical immunities aren't the only kind of protection we're to provide for our child. We're to concern ourselves with *spiritual* immunization as well—that is, protection for our little one's spiritual well-being. And what exactly might that involve?

Protecting your child's innocence—Romans 16:19 says, "I want you to be wise about what is good, and innocent about what is evil." First Thessalonians 5:21-22 (NKJV) says, "Test all things; hold fast what is good. Abstain from every form of evil." We are to encourage our children to embrace what is good and to shun evil. Some parents believe that the earlier we introduce a little one to the "grim realities" of this world, the better. We disagree, for doing so may end up causing a child to become unconcerned about negative influences—to the point of thinking there is nothing wrong with them.

Protecting your child's mind—As your children grow up, the world bombards them with negative thoughts about themselves and others. And temptation constantly beckons them toward compromise and sin. We can counter these influences by 1) affirming our children with the truth that they are loved and special, and 2) encouraging them to resist negative thoughts and temptation by focusing their minds on "whatever things are true, whatever things are noble, whatever things are just, whatever things are pure, whatever things are lovely, whatever things are of good report" (Philippians 4:8 NKJV).

Protecting your child's heart—Every human being is destined to eternity in either heaven or hell. The best way you can help your children in this battle for the heart is to introduce them to God and His Word as early as possible. Read to your children from a toddler's Bible, talk with them about God, and teach them the truths they need to know for making the right choices in life.

Making It Happen—If you haven't already done so, purchase a Bible storybook for babies/toddlers. Go to a local Christian bookstore and write a list of age-appropriate books, music CDs, and videos that will help protect your child's innocence, mind, and heart. Then buy one or two of these items every couple weeks or so. If your church library has such resources, make use of them. Ultimately, your goal is to help expose your child to as many biblical and positive influences as you can.

Dads and Sons, Dads and Daughters

So God created man in his own image,
in the image of God he created him;
male and female he created them.

(Genesis 1:27)

Dad, the way you father your child may differ according to the baby's gender. As the father of a son, you'll be a role model, a mentor, and, hopefully a good buddy. For your daughter, you'll model the kind of man she may want to marry someday. She will look to you for protection more than as a role model.

Your play will differ as well according to the sex of the child. While both boys and girls like to roughhouse with dad to some extent, it will be your son who enjoys the wrestling matches and games. Your daughter, on the other hand, will eventually invite you to the tea party she's having with her dolls. You'll attend, of course. And you'll let her know that her tea party is just as important to you as your game of touch football with Junior.

Much of what you need to know about the differences in parenting boys and girls will be learned on the job. You will instinctively know how to respond—if you're paying attention.

An important aspect of your fatherhood is to reinforce your child's gender. Mom can help with this, too. Both of you must cultivate a male spirit in your sons and a female spirit in your girls. Don't just assume it will happen. Nature usually takes its course as youngsters learn to identify properly with their assigned gender. But dad, this happens early as a child receives clues about his or her gender and identifies as a male or female according to those clues or signals.

Problems arise, though, when mom, dad, and society at large send mixed signals. These signals often relate to clothing, hair, toys, nicknames, and simply treating the child either gender-neutral or worse.

Respect the gender of each child God gives you...and teach each of them to do the same.

Making It Happen—Talk with your wife tonight about ways to gently reinforce your child's gender as he or she grows. If you were hoping for a child of the opposite sex, you may have to be doubly careful that neither of you reflect disappointment in the way you relate to the child God has given you.

Dad: The Source of Life

The LORD God formed the man from the dust of the ground and breathed into his nostrils the breath of life, and the man became a living being.

(GENESIS 2:7)

Ultimately all life originates in God—few Christians would dispute that. But, biologically speaking, on this earth, God uses fathers as the source of transmitting human life. From their body comes a living sperm that finds its way to the awaiting egg in the mother's body. The life of the sperm unites with the egg and…well, you've known all about this process since you were a boy.

But have you really considered the implications? You are the source of your child's life. His or her life originated with you. In fact, you were the determinant of your child's sex. Sure, without mom's egg, there would be no child. But the male carries the life and is usually the initiator in the sexual relationship.

And now that the baby's born, are you *still* the source of your baby's life? In a very real way, *yes*. Just as God's life is in us as Christians, so too is your life in your child. Part of you continues on down through time in your descendants. What a miracle!

And from a practical point of view, God continues to use you to supply life to your child through your role as provider, protector, and leader of your family. And in these tasks, a man finds his deepest joy. It was for this a male was created: to provide *life* for his family. Naturally, a Christian man depends on God to fulfill this charge. And the more he depends on God, the more successful a father he is.

You gave your child life through one act of love. Now continue to give life through continued acts of paternal love.

Making It Happen—Take a few moments and reflect on yourself as the source of life for your child. First biologically, but now as provider, protector, and sustainer. Clearly a baby left to himself would die very quickly. A baby is totally dependent on mom and dad for life. And dad, your duties are therefore indispensable in the healthy survival of your child. Without what you can provide, your child would grow stilted, disadvantaged, and with a huge hole in his or her life. That's how important you are.

The Perfect Father

*You, O L*ORD*, are our Father.*

(ISAIAH 63:16)

One of the more amusing traits of babies is that they often try to imitate their parents. They will copy our facial expressions, our body movements, and the sounds we make. And as our children grow older, they will copy our mannerisms, our words, and our actions. These attempts at imitation are actually good, for they help our children to develop and mature. That brings us to an important principle: Children do their best learning when they have a role model to watch—and you and your wife have the privilege of being the primary role models in your children's lives.

Not only do children benefit from role models, but adults do, too. As a new dad, I'm sure you've already experienced times when you wished you could have looked to another father for ideas on how to be a better parent. We all find ourselves in awkward situations where we're not sure what to do. That's why we need someone who can help us take steps in the right direction—someone who can serve as an example of how we can best...

- love our children

- lead our children by example

- be available for our children

- provide for our children

- show forgiveness toward our children

- protect our children

And dad, there's no better place to look for a role model than God Himself. He is the supreme example of what it means to be a father.

There is much we can learn about fatherhood simply by watching the way God interacts with His children. For example, when Adam and Eve rebelled and had to be expelled from the Garden, God still cared for them as a father. When Abraham lied to the Egyptians about his wife, Sarah, God still offered the couple His fatherly protection. When Jacob practiced deceit at the expense of others, God still paved the way to preserve Jacob's family and the young nation of Israel from a devastating famine that would have wiped them out. When Moses insisted he couldn't possibly lead the Israelites out of Egypt, God still expressed a fatherly confidence in Moses and stuck by him. When the Israelites refused to enter the Promised Land and God punished them with 40 years in the wilderness, He did not abandon them. He gave them food and water, preserved their clothing, and met the every need of some two million people all through those 40 years.

And on and on it goes. All through the Bible, we see God faithfully fulfilling His role as a heavenly Father who cares for His children. His faithfulness runs as an unbroken thread through even the darkest of nights and most difficult of circumstances. The message is clear: Even when God's children fail Him, He never fails His children.

That's the kind of father I want as a role model. How about you?

Making It Happen—In the next seven devotions, we will take a closer look at how we can learn from God's example as a Father. We'll learn several character traits that can equip us to be better fathers to our children. Pray and ask God to help you make these character traits real in your own life...so that your children may see clear glimpses of God in the things you say and do.

A Father Whose Love Never Changes

I will declare that your love stands firm forever.

(PSALM 89:2)

Ever have one of those days when you wondered how God could possibly still love you? When you made so many mistakes that you thought, *Surely God must be frustrated with me. I wouldn't blame Him if He wanted to disown me!*

As Christians, we may have times when we feel as if God is upset or angry with us. Perhaps it's because we don't read the Bible as we should, or because we keep falling into a particular sin again and again. In our minds, we may even imagine God withholding His love from us because we're not doing as well in our Christian life as we think we should.

But God's love doesn't work that way.

God's love for us is always constant. His love doesn't increase or decrease based on our performance as Christians. Consider what the Bible tells us:

Before you became a Christian, God loved you: "God demonstrates his own love for us in this: While we were still sinners, Christ died for us" (Romans 5:8). Two verses later, we read that before salvation, we were enemies of God. Ephesians 2 says we were "the sons of disobedience" and "by nature children of wrath" (verses 2-3 NKJV). Even when there was *nothing* redeeming about us, God showed His love to us.

God's love is constant: "Because of the LORD's great love we are not consumed, for his compassions never fail. They are new every morning; great is your faithfulness" (Lamentations 3:22-23). Not only is God's love unceasing, but He expresses it anew each day.

God's love goes to great lengths: In the book of Hosea, we read that the prophet Hosea married a woman named Gomer. She became a prostitute, bore illegitimate children, and left her husband. Later, when she was put up for sale on the slave market, Hosea bought her and lovingly took her back home. This account illustrates for us God's love for wayward Israel. God pleaded, "My heart is changed within me; all my compassion is aroused" (Hosea 11:8).

You may be asking, "But doesn't God grieve when we sin? Doesn't He express a righteous anger in response to our disobedience?" Yes He does. And yes, He will at times punish us as a father disciplines a child (see Hebrews 12:5-11). But God's anger and grief is manifest alongside a perfect love that longs for what is right and best for us.

It's this kind of love that we as fathers are to show our children. Though they may frustrate or grieve us, our love needs to be constant. Make sure your children know you love them—show it in your words, your actions, your faithfulness as a father. Dad, there's no better way to show your children that no matter what happens, they can count on you...and your love.

Making It Happen—What are five simple ways you can show your love for your child? Write your ideas on a 3 x 5 index card and use it as a bookmark in this book. Put these ideas to work this week, and begin making them a habit in your life. After you finish this book, place the list in your wallet or your Bible so you have a constant reminder of ways to show your fatherly love.

—

A Father Who Forgives

Be kind and compassionate to one another,
forgiving each other, just as in Christ God forgave you.

(EPHESIANS 4:32)

The human heart is very good at nursing grudges.

What's our first response when someone wrongs us? Vengeance of some sort. Sometimes our retaliation is immediate; other times we let our anger stew and plot revenge in our minds. Rarely is our first reaction one of forgiveness. Sometimes we will let hours, days, or even weeks go by, ignoring God's gentle whisper through our conscience that we need to let go of the offense and forgive the offender. The results are broken family relationships and friendships. A grudge is a wedge that divides, while forgiveness is a glue that binds.

Perhaps you have already experienced times when your little one has "wronged" you and you became upset. Perhaps your child's nighttime crying was depriving you of sleep. Or the infant's frequent need for attention interrupted the big game you were trying to watch on television. Or the baby just wouldn't cooperate, and you became irritated with him or her.

I remember when our firstborn son, Keith, battled with colic at night for several weeks. Pediatricians don't all agree on what causes colic, but all parents do agree that the crying spells, which can last all day or all night, can be both trying and tiring. I admit to getting so upset at times that instead of speaking gentle, soothing words that might help calm him, I would snap angrily at him to stop crying. But then God would convict me and remind me that Keith had no control over the colic. In fact, an infant's accidents or "harmful deeds" are rarely intentional. And even when they are, Scripture clearly commands us to be kind, compassionate, and forgiving.

When a child comes to us all covered with mud, we place him in the tub and wash him off. We get rid of the mud and not the child. In the same way, when we wrong God, His desire is to get rid of the sin, not us. What's more, when God forgives us, He does so completely. He doesn't dredge up the past at a later time: "As far as the east is from the west, so far has he removed our transgressions from us" (Psalm 103:12). If we forgive but don't "let it go," then we haven't really forgiven the other person.

When you are kind and forgiving, your children will learn how to be kind and forgiving as well. The result? You'll have a much happier family.

Making It Happen—Are there any grudges or frustrations you've harbored against someone near to you? Confess them to the Lord, and ask Him to help you be kind and compassionate even when your patience is sorely tried. It won't be easy, but the extra effort will mean family relationships that are close-knit rather than frayed.

---✕✕✕---

A Father Who Is Accessible

*Let us then approach the throne of grace
with confidence, so that we may receive mercy
and find grace to help us in our time of need.*

(HEBREWS 4:16)

On a hot day in Manhattan in July 1981, in a room brimming with several dozen journalists and a number of TV cameras, the then-chairman of a media company opened a much-anticipated press conference with these words: "I'm here to announce the launch of an exciting new concept in cable television. By this time next year, we'll be offering the nation's first all-weather television programming. It will be all weather, twenty-four hours a day. We call it…The Weather Channel."

The response?

> First, silence. Then a collective groan went up from the audience. And from the tone of the questions that followed, it became all too clear what those groans meant…. Isn't twenty-four hours a day of weather going to be, well, dull? Who will actually watch this stuff?[6]

The Weather Channel almost never made it. But some 20-plus years later, it's one of the more phenomenal success stories of cable television with a following well into the millions. The Weather Channel is successful for many reasons, but a big part of its success can be explained in just one word: access.

With The Weather Channel, people nationwide can get weather news whenever they want it. And to the more than 10 million people in the United States who travel more than 100 miles every day,[7] weather information is of great importance. If a cable TV or computer is handy, you can get a report for any place in America—instantly. *That's* accessibility!

Yet when it comes to accessibility, no one can outdo our heavenly Father. We can come to Him at any time, anywhere, for any reason. Speaking of God's ever-presence in our lives, King David said, "If I go up to the heavens, you are there; if I make my bed in the depths, you are there. If I rise on the wings of the dawn, if I settle on the far side of the sea, even there your hand will guide me" (Psalm 139:8-10).

God is a Father who is always there for us. That's why the writer of Hebrews encourages us, saying, "Let us then approach the throne of grace with confidence, so that we may receive mercy and find grace to help us in our time of need" (4:16). To God, there is no such thing as an interruption. He is always ready to welcome us into His presence.

Dad, do you make yourself accessible to your little one? While your job and household responsibilities may keep you busy at times, still, are you doing what you can to give your child the confidence that he or she can come to you at any time for any reason? For a child, having such a confidence provides a wonderful sense of security and love that will go far in keeping you close to one another.

Making It Happen—Thank your heavenly Father for His accessibility. Ask Him to help you be sensitive and make yourself available at times when your child has a need. Also, make sure you set aside time each day just to be with your child—to talk, to play, to listen. Do this so it becomes a habit.

A Father Who Is Holy

Just as he who called you is holy, so be holy in all you do;
for it is written: "Be holy, because I am holy."

(1 PETER 1:15-16)

There's no denying the power of a good example. While this is true in every area of life, we find it especially evident in sports. It's the outstanding athletes who, by their example, inspire the rest of the team or their fellow competitors toward better performance. We're talking about the Mary Lou Rettons, the Joe Montanas, the Wayne Gretzkys, the Kobe Bryants, the Tiger Woodses.

What's intriguing is that these athletes inspire not by their words but by their lives. Just by watching them in action, we wish we could have that same swing, throw, twirl, dunk, or stride. We find ourselves awed by their abilities and drawn to watch them again and again even though we've already seen them in action a multitude of times.

Holiness can inspire in a similar way. Have you ever watched someone else make a right choice in a moral dilemma, and been inspired to do likewise? Have you ever found yourself strengthened to resist falling into sin when a fellow believer said no to temptation? The apostle Paul recognized the power of a positive example when he said, "Follow my example, as I follow the example of Christ" (1 Corinthians 11:1). He knew how one Christian can inspire another toward greater spiritual growth.

As a dad, you have the greatest opportunity to be a positive example. When it comes to the choices you make in life, the apostle Paul said it best: "Do not offer the parts of your body to sin...but rather offer yourselves to God...and offer the parts of your body to him as instruments of righteousness" (Romans 6:13). Are you yielding yourself to God? Are you allowing Him to empower you?

Yes, sometimes we give in to temptation. When we do, we cannot blame anyone but ourselves, for God promises a way of escape—"he will not let you be tempted beyond what you can bear" (1 Corinthians 10:13). Yet when we fall, God stands nearby, ready to help us up, waiting for us to yield ourselves to Him and allow His Spirit to work through us. Galatians 5:16 puts it very simply: When we "walk in the Spirit," we will "not fulfill the lust of the flesh" (NKJV). Who is it that empowers us? The Spirit. And what is our role? To walk, or submit. The result? The Spirit's fruit will be manifest through us (Galatians 5:22-23). And when the Spirit's fruit shines through our lives, others become inspired to grow in those qualities as well—including our children.

While there's pleasure and a certain level of gratification that your children will get as they emulate the athletes, performers, peers, and others who inspire them in one way or another, they'll experience their greatest level of fulfillment as they're inspired toward Christ and spiritual growth...through *your* example.

Making It Happen—Look at the fruit of the Spirit in Galatians 5:22-23. What are some spiritual qualities you would like to inspire in your child's life? Take a moment in prayer to thank the Lord for His enablement in your life...and ask Him to keep you mindful of the fact that you, as a father, will have a powerful influence on the little life following your footsteps.

A Father Who Protects

The LORD is my rock, my fortress and my deliverer;
my God is my rock, in whom I take refuge.

(2 SAMUEL 22:2-3)

When the weather turns nasty, our first instinct is to run for shelter. And if conditions are really bad—such as when a tornado or hurricane threatens to wreak havoc—we'll take additional precautions, such as shuttering up the house, securing loose objects, and heading for the basement. Without shelter, we feel vulnerable and endangered; within a shelter, we feel safe and secure.

In our sin-plagued world, life is one constant storm. We have a determined enemy, Satan, who desires to batter us from all sides. Every day, we encounter people who hurt and disappoint us for one reason or another. And we're constantly faced with circumstances that are beyond our control, where things go wrong, fall apart, and can't be fixed.

It's at times like these that we, as children of God, can run into our heavenly Father's arms and seek refuge in the midst of all that threatens us. He will protect us, shield us, and lovingly guide us through whatever it is that besets us:

- We wait in hope for the LORD; he is our help
  and our shield (Psalm 33:20).

- God is our refuge and strength, an ever-present help in trouble (Psalm 46:1).

- In you my soul takes refuge. I will take refuge in the shadow of your wings until the disaster has passed (Psalm 57:1).

- He is my refuge and my fortress, my God, in whom I trust (Psalm 91:2).

- You have been a refuge for the poor, a refuge for the needy in his distress, a shelter from the storm and a shade from the heat (Isaiah 25:4).

- He is a shield to those who take refuge in him (Proverbs 30:5).

As your children grow up, they'll receive their first exposure to the different storms they'll encounter in life. In some of these "first encounters," they will likely experience fear and uncertainty. Will they know they can run to you for protection and help? Will they know that when the going gets rough, you'll help make it smooth? Will they know that they can count on you at all times?

We as Christians are assured of all those things by our heavenly Father. And we as earthly fathers can make sure our children feel that very same assurance from us.

Making It Happen—Think back to a time when you were facing difficult circumstances. How did you feel then? Did you eventually seek your heavenly Father's help and protection? If so, how did you feel afterward? Pray and thank God for being an ever-present refuge for you. Pray also for Him to give you the sensitivity and wisdom that will enable you to be a similar refuge for your children.

A Father Who Provides

God will meet all your needs
according to his glorious riches in Christ Jesus.

(Philippians 4:19)

There is one airline meal I will never forget. Not because of how pitiful it was, but how unexpected it was.

It was late afternoon, and I'd had an extremely busy day. I'd had no lunch, so my body was running on fumes, feeling utterly depleted. I had gone straight from work to the airport, and I looked forward to dinner on the flight.

While I was waiting for the airplane, however, a flight attendant quickly strode into the terminal and announced the flight had been delayed. It was the last flight out, which meant I wouldn't reach my destination that night. Then the attendant added, "There's an alternate flight on another airline, but it's leaving right now, so you'll have to hurry." I immediately asked where to go, and the attendant pointed, then warned, "You won't be served dinner on that flight. They won't have any spare meals available." I winced at this news, but I also knew I didn't have much choice if I wanted to get to my destination.

Oddly enough, I was the only person who chose to take the alternate flight. I was assigned a seat at the back of the plane, and by this time I was famished. When the time came to serve the meals, the attendants started at the front of the plane and worked their way back. I knew there wouldn't be a spare meal available and had already resigned myself to that reality. But the aroma in the air and the sight of meals being handed out didn't help any.

Some minutes later, an attendant reached into the meal cart and pulled out what was clearly the last meal, intended for the man across from me. With a gracious smile, she offered it to him. He hesitated for a moment, then looked up to her and said, "No, thanks." The woman stood for a moment as if uncertain what to do; she knew I had come aboard from another airline. Then she turned and said, "You want it?" It was all I could do to restrain myself from gushing a huge sigh of relief. I did my best to give a modest, "Sure, thanks"—but deep inside, I felt over-whelmed. I had not expected this at all. This was clearly God's provision. He saw my need, and He met it. What was especially fitting is that each meal was served with a slip of paper featuring a beautiful photo and a Bible verse. It read, "I will praise God's name in song and glorify Him with thanksgiving" (Psalm 69:30). I still have that slip—it's a perpetual reminder that God will provide, and that I never have reason to worry.

While an airline meal may seem a trivial thing, believe me, at that time, it wasn't. To me it affirmed that our Father in heaven cares for us in the little things as well as the big. And we, as earthly fathers, are called to do the same for our child. May we be ever watchful to note our child's needs—no matter how triv-ial they may appear. To a child, no need is a small thing. And as you show that you care, he or she will come to know he or she can count on you...in the same way that we can count on God.

Making It Happen—What are some of the needs your baby has each day? Do you find yourself eager to meet those needs, fulfilling them cheerfully? Memorize Philippians 4:19, and let this truth about our heavenly Father encour-age you in your role as a father.

—

A Father Who Is Faithful

The one who calls you is faithful and he will do it.

(1 THESSALONIANS 5:24)

One of the more hallowed sports records an athlete can hold is that of most consecutive games played. In football, Jim Marshall, a former Cleveland Brown and Minnesota Viking, holds the record with 282 games. When A.C. Green of the Los Angeles Lakers retired, he was several hundred games ahead of the next active NBA player, with 1192 consecutive games played. But the record that captured the attention of an entire nation in the summer of 1996 was the one in Major League Baseball—when Cal Ripken clipped Lou Gehrig's seemingly unsurpassable consecutive-games record and continued to play till he reached 2632 games. From May 30, 1982, to September 19, 1998, he played every single game—an impressive record indeed.

Yet even the greatest records of all are a drop in the bucket compared to God's track record for keeping His promises. Simply put, God has never failed to keep a promise. Noah waited 120 years for the worldwide flood. Abraham and Sarah waited some 30 years for the son promised to them. The people of Israel waited 40 years in the wilderness before they entered the Promised Land. The Jewish people waited again, this time for 70 years, during the Babylonian captivity. The Old Testament prophets proclaimed Christ's first coming 500 to 1000 years before God fulfilled His promise. In fact, the first prophecy of Christ's birth goes back to Genesis 3:15—thousands of years before it happened.

In every case, God fulfilled His promise. The rise and fall of kingdoms didn't stop Him. The fact that millions of people through history have refused to cooperate with Him didn't stop Him. Neither could the passage of time stop Him—even time measuring into the thousands of years.

No matter what the promise, we can count on God to fulfill it. Promises such as...

- The eyes of the Lord are on the righteous and his ears are attentive to their prayers (1 Peter 3:12).

- Call upon me in the day of trouble; I will deliver you (Psalm 50:15).

- Cast your burden on the LORD, and he will sustain you (Psalm 55:22).

- I am with you always (Matthew 28:20).

- If any of you lacks wisdom, he should ask God (James 1:5).

- I give [my sheep] eternal life, and they shall never perish; no one can snatch them out of my hand (John 10:28).

There's a story told about a boy whose dad dropped him off at a street corner. The father told his son to be there in half an hour when he returned. But the father's car broke down, and he couldn't get back to his son at the appointed time. In fact, hours went by. The father worried that his son might be frightened, wondering where he was. When the father finally returned, he hugged his son and apologized profusely and asked, "Weren't you worried?" The boy answered, "No, Dad. You said you would come, and I knew you would."

Dad, isn't that the kind of faithfulness you'd like to be known for…in things both big and small?

Making It Happen—Write a list of the ways you can show faithfulness to your wife and baby. Save that list for a month, and review it each day. Are you growing in your displays of faithfulness? Let your list serve as an encouragement to make faithfulness a habit in your life.

Dads in Our Culture

Honor your father and your mother,
so that you may live long in the land the
LORD your God is giving you.

(EXODUS 20:12)

Have you noticed how dads generally fare in our culture these days? On TV, most dads are depicted as bozos married to wise women who must basically mother their husbands. She's always right, he seldom is. And in many cases, dad is deemed totally unnecessary. And the movies aren't any better.

Not too many years ago, good dads were "in" culturally. But then something happened. Amidst objections that such dads were a rarity, the pendulum swung. Dads became losers. Jerks. Adolescents. Even animated dads, such as Homer Simpson, are portrayed as ineffectual or worse.

Guys, this is fiction—big time. Don't buy into this cultural shift that demeans dads…that demeans *you* and your God-assigned role. Turn off the TV when your role as a man is under attack. Don't go to movies that portray men as immoral self-seekers (and these are often the good guys!). Help turn the tide and restore the position of father to a place of honor and respect. If you don't, you will soon begin to accept these cultural messages that emasculate fatherhood. You will doubt your abilities as a dad, and your kids will surely pick up your lack of esteem and confidence. *What you believe about yourself as a dad will influence what your children will believe.*

Tragically, a lot of the problems we face as a society are rooted in the destruction of fatherhood and the ensuing breakup of the family. And unless you are aware of the assault and resist, your family will be affected by this antifamily virus.

Celebrate fatherhood—enjoy being a man in an antifamily culture. Fulfill your role with joy. Don't be robbed of your family. Stand out as a light in a dark world.

Making It Happen—Keep your remote by your chair (I know, I know…it's already there) and change channels when dad is under assault. If you're really motivated, write the networks and sponsors of the programs you're no longer watching and tell them why. And don't forget to commend *good* programming when you see it.

A Child's Temperament

Every good and perfect gift is from above,
coming down from the father of the heavenly lights,
who does not change like shifting shadows.

(JAMES 1:17)

Like the oft-cited snowflake, no two children are like. A family of three sons may have three totally different boys—ranging from the athletic jock to the science whiz to the sensitive artist. Three daughters may include the princess, the scholar, and the tomboy.

A wise father *expects* differences in his children and, from the birth of the child, watches for ways to help his child develop and become a good steward of whatever gifts God has given him or her. One of your primary roles, then, is to be your child's *encourager.*

Sure, it's one of fatherhood's great blessings to pass on to our children the same interests we have. Ball games, piano recitals, trips to the library, and political conventions are all great ways to share our passions with our children. However, too often a dad expects a certain type of temperament or interest from his child and then registers open disappointment when the child doesn't express that same interest in his favorite pastimes.

If you were interested in sports as a boy, you may expect more athletic ability from your son than he's able to deliver. And while it's true that if you're closely bonded to your son, he *is* more likely to enjoy the same things you do—it's not *always* true. You aren't failing as a father when your child exhibits personality traits and interests that are different from yours. If you're musical and your child isn't, don't force him or her to excel in piano lessons.

Many fathers are naturally fix-it men. They love to diagnose problems, search for solutions, and implement the necessary changes. But when it comes to the temperament of your child, there's no fixing necessary. A good father will help *shape* the natural temperament of his child...but he will do so out of respect for the uniqueness of the child.

Watch and see just what kind of gift God has given you in the temperament of your child. Accept it, find the appropriate opportunities to direct your child into, and *love* the differences.

Making It Happen—Thank God for giving you *this* child. Thank Him for whatever gifts and talents He has planned for this little one. Determine to value this child no matter what his or her temperament or interests may turn out to be.

Let your love be like your heavenly Father's— the One who has given you this "good and perfect gift" of a child. Be like Him—don't let your love change like shifting shadows.

When You're Away from Home

Though I am absent from you in body,
I am present with you in spirit.

(COLOSSIANS 2:5)

Babies are far more aware of what's happening around them than we give them credit for. Studies have shown that infants can readily discern the voices of their parents from the voices of others at a very early age. Studies also show that babies are not only highly aware of their parents' presence at any given time, but they can also be affected by their mom and dad's absence.

Our every contact with our infant child throughout the day is one more small strand that, over time, builds a strong cord of bonding in the parent-child relationship. Yet an unfortunate reality for many of us dads is that we sometimes have to be away from home for an extended period of time—whether our job requires it or special circumstances call for us to be gone.

Just because you're away from home, however, doesn't mean you have to be "away" from your child. Here are some ways you can continue to nurture your parent-child relationship even while you're on the road:

- Read some bedtime stories aloud onto a cassette tape. While you're gone, your wife can play portions of the tape to your child each night at bedtime.

- If you have a video camera, tape several short greetings and messages that can be played back one at a time each morning and evening that you're gone.

- Place a framed picture of you and your wife near your child's crib (not within reach of your child's hands, of course). Each morning and night, mommy can show the picture to baby and, pointing at you, say, "Good morning, daddy" and "Good night, daddy."

- Write a postcard or short letter to your baby and mail it home while you're gone. Then mommy can read the card or note, saying it's from daddy.

- When you're able, call home and have your wife hold the phone to your baby's ear so you can talk to him or her.

These little touches—your voice on tape, your smile on a video clip, your voice on the phone, and more—will provide a "continuity of contact" that you otherwise wouldn't have. And as you plan ahead for the days when you're gone, you'll find it's actually quite fun to come up with creative ways to keep in touch with your baby!

Making It Happen—Just for fun, why not tape a short story on cassette for your child in the next day or two, and have your wife play it while you're gone at work or doing errands? Not only will this give your spouse and child a special activity they can do together, but you can make the tape a part of your "care package" for the next time you have to travel.

———

Dad, the Good Steward

*Those who have been given a trust
must prove faithful.*

(1 CORINTHIANS 4:2)

A steward is someone who looks after something that belongs to another. God has given mankind stewardship over many things: the earth, our bodies, our finances, the gospel, and our families.

And yet many Christian parents fail as stewards of their children. I call this "reverse evangelism." If we labor to win others to Christ yet neglect our own family, we will lose our children to the world when they're adults.

Several years ago my wife and I attended a church filled with very committed believers. We were (we thought) committed to each other as brothers and sisters in the Lord, committed to reaching others for Christ, and certainly committed to the church we attended. But as time went by, my wife and I noticed a very alarming pattern: Most—not just many, but *most*—of the kids in the church were growing up and not only leaving the church but also abandoning their faith.

I asked one of these young adults why this had happened to them. "After all," I said, "your parents are earnest Christians. They really love the Lord." My young friend replied, "Yes, it's true—our whole family was centered around the church. We were there every time the doors were open. But that was the problem. Our parents only saw us as extensions of their church work. They never set aside time for just *us*."

Many busy Christian workers—ministers, missionaries, Sunday school teachers—have been so busy with church that they've not been faithful stewards over their most important trust: their children.

I don't know how active you are in your church. You may be simply a regular attender or you may be a pastor or youth leader...but you must make your family your first priority, even over ministry. Family must come first. *Must come first!* God won't be impressed with all your good works if you have failed with your children.

To be really zealous for the Lord, be zealous for your children.

Making It Happen—Write a list of your major responsibilities. Put them in their present order of the time and money they require from you. Include your job, church responsibilities, professional organizations, hobbies, service clubs, school, and of course, your family.

After you've written your list, look at it. Do the demands on your life appear in the order that they should be in? How can you begin the process of rearranging them in a better sequence? Are there some activities that are a drain on your time without returning a profit worthy of that time?

You may have to say no to some things for a while. In so doing, you say yes to your family—and to God.

The Influence of Grandparents

I thank God...when I call to remembrance
the genuine faith that is in you, which dwelt first
in your grandmother Lois and your mother Eunice...

(2 TIMOTHY 1:3,5 NKJV)

The apostle Paul wrote the words above to Timothy, whose introduction to God and Christianity apparently had much to do with his grandmother, Lois, and his mother, Eunice. This is a clear affirmation of the valuable influence grandparents can have on children. As family, your parents and your in-laws will have a significant interest in your baby's well-being, and you will find them a wonderful source of love, wisdom, and interaction for your child.

Grandparents sometimes have their own ideas about how to take care of a baby, and this can become a source of friction—but it doesn't need to. When it comes to feeding, dressing, and playing with your little one, you as the parents need to set the rules. Do make it clear to your parents and in-laws that you appreciate their help, but gently let them know you would like them to abide by your requests. Consistency in care-taking patterns helps your baby to know what to anticipate and to feel secure. Inconsistency, by contrast, can cause confusion and give conflicting messages to a baby. When it comes to communicating your desires to the grandparents, here's a simple guideline: You take care of your own parents, and your spouse takes care of hers.

Remember, too, that grandparents *want* to feel wanted. They enjoy watching and participating in your baby's growth as much as you do, and deep in their hearts, they want to have the kind of relationship with your child that makes them a significant part of his or her life. So take time to think of ways to let the grandparents be involved. Don't merely use them as baby-sitters, but invite them to participate in some of your family activities, such as trips to the park or beach. If the grandparents live far away, take pictures frequently and send them in the mail....or have your baby "talk" on the phone with them. If they have Internet access, you can even hold your baby's hands and guide him or her in typing a sentence or two in an e-mail to grandma and grandpa. Make sure to involve the grandparents on *both* sides of the family to avoid arousing jealousy.

When you take extra steps to involve the grandparents, you'll be providing your child with a greater sense of family and an additional source of love and guidance. Every positive influence on your child's life counts—especially in this day of numerous negative influences. As the Bible tells us, it made a difference in Timothy's life—to the point of leading him to Christ—and it can make a difference in your child's life, too.

Making It Happen—Want to give your parents and in-laws some great ideas for their role as grandparents? As a gift, give them the book *Grandloving: Making Memories with Your Grandchildren* by Sue Johnson and Julie Carlson (Fairport, NY: Heartstrings Press, 2000). This book is filled with all kinds of great suggestions for inexpensive and memorable activities grandparents can do with their grandchildren.

Playtime

The city streets will be filled
with boys and girls playing there.

(ZECHARIAH 8:5)

Okay, I confess. One of my secret delights as my girls were born was the fun I knew I'd have playing with them. Having children allowed me to be a child again myself. I could hardly wait to get out the blocks and Tinker Toys from my own child-hood. To my surprise, my daughters wanted to play with *dolls*. Well, I had an adjustment to make. The Tinker Toys, blocks, and racing cars were put away.

No, I didn't take up dolls as a hobby...but I did learn to join in their fun as best I could—starting early. Simple finger games at first, like "Itsy-Bitsy Spider" and patty-cake, later gave way to hide-and-seek, I spy, and board games like Candy Land®.

Dad, be inventive in playing with your growing baby. Just remember, this tot's not ready yet for the raucous roughhousing that will come in a few years. Keep your play simple and fun. Don't expect too much except the delightful giggles and coos from your happy baby. At this tender age, the best fun for your baby will be seeing your creative facial expressions. You can gradually increase your effectiveness as the best toy in the house by looking for simple ways to elicit a smile—gently splashing the water in his or her bath, lightly tugging or tickling (don't overdo it) on the feet, and of course, making even *more* creative faces.

Eventually you'll find unique ways to delight your young one. For me, it was the tummy blow. That's where I'd puff up my cheeks as if to blow up a balloon and instead put my mouth on the baby's tummy and let out the air out as fast as I could, creating one long *SPLAAATTT.*

There's simply nothing like play to bond with your child. God invented fun. Enjoy!

Making It Happen—Gently play around with the baby at an appropriate time (not right after nursing or a nap), making faces and noises you wouldn't be caught dead making anywhere else. At as little as two months, the baby will respond with throaty noises that are precursors to an eventual laugh, which could come as early as four months.

Forming Your Child's Identity

You are all sons of God through faith in Christ Jesus,
for all of you who were baptized into Christ
have clothed yourselves with Christ.

(GALATIANS 3:26-27)

Right from the get-go, children start to form their identity from the signals they receive from mom and dad. Where else can they learn who they are and what their place is in the world? Kids who grow up without a clear sense of their identity can often trace their confusion to a failure on the part of mom, and especially dad, to affirm this identity.

From the very beginning of the Bible, in the book of Genesis, we're told about a very important part of our identity as human beings—we are created in the image of God. And after giving us such a fantastic start on a good self-image, God continues to affirm the identity of His people throughout the Bible. Over and over again He restates His love and care for us. It is, in fact, in reading the Word that we grow in our identity as God's children. We simply need to hear over and over again of who we are in Christ. And the apostle Paul certainly obliges us. Verse after verse reminds us of our unchangeable identity as sons of God. *Sons of God!* We dads are too easily robbed of our worth in God's eyes. And because we often are not secure in who we are, we neglect to pass along a strong sense of identity to our children.

Dad, it's in your job specs to help form your child's identity. And with your newborn, this starts by sending signals of his or her worth. You can speak powerful words of acceptance and love to your child, even if the baby is only days old. He or she won't understand the words, of course, but you're starting something. You're establishing a pattern, a habit of affirming the sacredness of this life—and your words will continue to shape and encourage your child for all the years he or she will live.

And dad, even though mom can do this too, there's something unique and powerful when *you* do it. Your words to your child carry power—the power of acceptance or rejection.

Making It Happen—Start a list of words that you will never use directed toward your child. Here are some to start with:

- hate

- failure

- stupid

- clumsy

Take it from there. What words were directed at you as a child that you can add to the list?

Is Your Baby Sick?

I pray that you may enjoy good health.

(3 John 2)

Because infants are so little and fragile, even the simplest of illnesses can become serious quickly. The sooner you detect something is wrong, the better. However, because babies can't communicate what's happening to their bodies, figuring out if medical attention is needed can be tricky. When it comes to your baby's health, the most important rule is this: When in doubt, call the pediatrician. No question is a dumb question when your child's safety might be at stake.

You as a parent will usually be able to sense when your child doesn't feel well. Without even trying, you've probably become familiar with your little one's normal behaviors throughout the day. It's when your child acts different than usual that you should pay closer attention.

Here is a short list of signs to watch for:

- Is your child listless? Do you notice a lack of responsiveness? Are his or her eyes vacant or bloodshot?

- Has your baby lost his or her appetite?

- Is he or she crying more than usual or more irritable than normal?

- Does your baby want to be carried all the time?

- Is he or she laboring to breathe?

- Does he or she have a fever? If you're not sure, use a baby thermometer. An ear thermometer is very handy and easy to use.

- Is your baby's skin more pale than usual, or does he or she have reddish skin or a rash? Is any part of the body swollen?

- Has your baby had trouble sleeping?

- Has your baby vomited (rather than the usual spitting that accompanies burping)? Has diarrhea been an ongoing problem?

With any of the signs above, it's always good to seek advice from a doctor. Your responsibility as a parent is not to figure out *what* is wrong, but to determine *if* something is wrong.

And before sickness strikes, prepare yourself by having at least three or four phone numbers handy in case you need help. Ask your doctor or pediatrician whom you can call at night or during weekends. Planning ahead is the best kind of preventative medicine and will save you a lot of anxiety when the time comes to seek medical attention for your baby.

Making It Happen—Do you have your doctor or pediatrician's phone numbers where you can access them immediately? What about a hospital number? Write three lists of phone numbers to call at daytime, nighttime, and during the weekend. Keep one list in your wallet, have your wife put one in her purse, and place a list next to the main telephone in your home.

Strong, Yet Tender

Be kind one to another, tenderhearted...

(EPHESIANS 4:32 NKJV)

During the American Civil War, many officers and generals distinguished themselves by carrying out their duties with exceptional courage and skill. And among this elite group, Robert E. Lee stands as one of the most respected of all. Military historians describe him as a brilliant strategist and bold commander who won key victories in the face of overwhelming odds. Lee's own soldiers loved their general dearly, revering him as a valiant leader, a true man's man on the battlefield.

But what makes Lee more special is the fact that during his long and arduous military career, he never set aside his fatherly love and tenderness. In his home, while with his children, he was a father, not a general. Consider these words from poetess Margaret J. Preston:

> His tenderness to his children, especially to his daughters, was mingled with a delicate courtesy which belonged to an older day than ours, a courtesy which recalls the *preux chevalier* of knightly times. He had a pretty way of addressing his daughters, in the presence of other people, with a prefix which would seem to

belong to the age of lace ruffles and side swords. "Where is my little Mildred?" he would say on coming home from his ride or walk at dusk. "She is my light-bearer; the house is never dark if she is in it."[8]

In these words we see Lee's love, respect, and even admiration for his children. Lee was a man and father who demonstrated both strength and tenderness.

Dad, what do you want to be known for? Consider these words from General Douglas MacArthur, yet another outstanding military general known for manly courage:

By profession I am a soldier and take pride in that fact. But I am prouder—infinitely prouder —to be a father. A soldier destroys in order to build; the father only builds, never destroys....It is my hope that my son, when I am gone, will remember me not from the battle field but in the home repeating with him our simple daily prayer, "Our Father who art in heaven."

Is that your wish as well?

Making It Happen—Take a moment in prayer now to ask God to make you a well-rounded father who expresses a tender side to his children. Ask the Lord to frequently remind you of what really counts in the father-child relationship —that you display a love and tenderness that provides your child with a sense of comfort and security, complemented with leadership and wisdom to make careful decisions, honor God, and do what is right and best for the family.

A Father's Power in Prayer

*Then he blessed Joseph and said, "May the God before whom my
fathers Abraham and Isaac walked, the God who has been my
shepherd all my life to this day, the Angel who has delivered me
from all harm—may he bless these boys. May they be called by
my name and the names of my fathers Abraham and Isaac, and
may they increase greatly upon the earth."*

(Genesis 48:15-16)

From antiquity, fathers have blessed their children in prayer.
In the verses above, we see the prayer of Israel over his son
Joseph. God answered that prayer...as He loves to do with
fathers from all ages.

A dad is called by God to be a prayer warrior for his child.
Prayer is a dad's number one tool for successful fatherhood.
Nothing will take its place. A dad who can't be with his child as
often as he'd like can still daily, faithfully, powerfully *pray* for his
child. Even a dad who's active in his child's life daily still must
pray.

God desires to accomplish His will on earth in response to
the prayers of His people. Our children can prosper if we dads
will simply pray for them. Ultimately prayers for our children
take root and spread: We soon find ourselves praying for
ourselves as fathers, for our wives as moms, for our communi-
ties, for our nation.

Dad, I may not know how busy you are. But I *do* know you're
not too busy to intercede with God for your child.

Making It Happen—Here are some ways you can begin to pray:

1. Offer gratitude for your role as the father of this child.

2. Ask God to protect your son or daughter from illness, accident, or other injurious events.

3. Pray for your son or daughter to have a strong spiritual sensitivity and to come to know Christ early.

4. Pray for your child to be used by God for His purposes throughout the child's life.

5. Start praying now for this child's mate. I know it seems a tad premature to pray for someone whom your son or daughter may not even meet for at least 20 years. Pray anyway. Ask God to set that special child aside for your son or daughter. Testimonies abound from fathers who have successfully prayed for the mates for their children for many years. And I'm one of them.

Dad, if this sounds like a lot of prayer, and you don't consider yourself much of a pray-er, then take each item and simply offer one request daily.

If you will be a Christian dad, you will find time to grow that child's life from your knees. God will bless.

Looking in the Mirror

Do not be deceived: God cannot be mocked. A man reaps what he sows. The one who sows to please his sinful nature, from that nature will reap destruction; the one who sows to please the Spirit, from the Spirit will reap eternal life.

(GALATIANS 6:7-8)

When we wake up each morning, we trudge sleepily to our bathroom mirror and see our own aging reflection peering back at us. This mirror we know and understand, sometimes liking what we see, sometimes less than satisfied with the man on the other side.

The new arrival at your house will also prove to be a very effective mirror for you in the years ahead. Your child, without exception, will reflect back to you what he or she sees you do. Your child will speak what you speak. (Have you ever heard Franklin Graham? Wow—he sounds just like his dad, the great evangelist.) If you speak without honor to your wife or your own parents, then your son or daughter will learn to talk disrespectfully to you. In just about every way, your children will reflect your own attitudes—good and bad—back to you.

The implications of this are enormous. More than ever, you must be the man of God you were always meant to be. Honor, integrity, moral purity, clean language, and respectful attitudes have just jumped up several notches on your list of priorities.

Perhaps it's in God's wisdom that our children mirror us. As in all of life, so in fathering—we will reap what we sow. Take care that your seeds are the right seeds.

Making It Happen—Dad, consider your relationship with your own parents for a minute. What are some of the attitudes, gestures, or even physical resemblances that you've picked up from your dad? How about from your mother? Have these all been good qualities...or are you a mirror reflecting some of the vices you saw in your parents?

Planning for the College Years

Suppose one of you wants to build a tower.
Will he not first sit down and estimate the cost
to see if he has enough money to complete it?

(LUKE 14:28)

Just yesterday, at the time of this writing, we got a letter in the mail that we cannot believe has finally arrived. Our oldest son, Keith, turned 18 years old last month, and it's now time to close the mutual fund account we established for his college savings because the account has matured. For years it seemed as if this day was so far away that it would never arrive. But it has…and we're shaking our heads with amazement. And Nathan is close behind, with just another two years to go!

Upon opening the letter, we were both glad and disappointed. Glad because the invested money will definitely prove helpful, and disappointed because we wish we could have set aside more through the years.

Our original goal was to open the fund by Keith's first birthday, but we delayed simply because money was very, very tight. And when at last we were able to open his college account, we found it difficult to add to it regularly.

If you're in the same predicament, do the best you can. The sooner you start, the better. And even a small amount is better than nothing. That's because the earnings from interest can grow quite quickly. For example, if you start during your child's first year, $40 a month for 18 years, at 11 percent interest, will add up to about $30,000. Or $25 a month at a meager 5 percent interest will grow to about $10,000 in 18 years. Even if all you can do is scrape together $10 a month, at 8 percent interest, you'll have $5,000 saved up. That may not seem like much when you consider the cost of an education, but don't let that discourage you. Every little bit *will* help!

You can also invite family members to contribute money on your child's birthday or at Christmastime. (I'll never forget the Christmas a cousin gave our middle son, Nathan, some money to set aside for college. I encouraged Nathan to write a thank-you card and told him to tell the cousin the money would go toward his college fund. Nathan was little at the time and his spelling wasn't all that great. He wrote, "Thank you for the money. I'm going to save it for my college fun.")

You may feel embarrassed about how little you can afford to set aside. Don't worry—that's your private business. Again, a little is better than nothing. And, the money *will* grow. Every little bit of progress now will mean a lot more progress later on.

Before you know it, you'll receive a letter like the one we just got. Our hope is that when you open it, you'll experience the satisfaction that comes from knowing you did all you could, no matter what your circumstances. That's a great feeling to have.

Making It Happen—This week, sit with your spouse and, with a look at your budget, try to agree on a plan. Determine how much you can set aside each month and investigate the investment options (CNNMoney is a helpful website that answers many questions about saving up for college; you'll find it at http://money.cnn.com). Agree with one another that you will start this savings plan in the next 30 to 60 days—if not sooner!

Praying for Your Child's Future

I have not stopped giving thanks for you,
remembering you in my prayers.

(Ephesians 1:16)

Have you already started to pray for your baby to someday find the right person to marry? To cultivate the right friendships in school? To possess a lifelong passion for the things of God? For wisdom in pursuing a career path?

There will be days when you find yourself saying, "It's all I can do just to pray for the patience and strength I need to survive one more day of keeping up with my child! Besides, isn't there plenty of time to pray for things that won't happen for 15 or 20 years?"

While we should always bring our immediate needs to the Lord in prayer, we will also find it beneficial to occasionally consider our child's future and lift those needs to the Lord in prayer as well. As we develop a sensitivity to what could happen in the days ahead, we will take advantage of certain "stepping stones" that will lead us to the final destination. For example, as we pray for our child's future spouse, we will become more mindful of teaching our child how to cultivate friendships and be thoughtful and considerate of others. As we pray for our child's salvation and relationship with God, we become more aware of everyday opportunities to sing or talk to our child about God.

When we pray for our child's future, we benefit in these ways:

- We learn to look at our child from God's perspective and be more open to the direction He might plan for his or her life (rather than relying on our own perspective, which is imperfect, has no knowledge of the future, and can sometimes be selfish).

- We are reminded to trust God to work out the details of His plans for our child (rather than try to work out those details ourselves).

- We are prompted to become fully dependent upon God for the wisdom and strength we need to raise our child through adulthood.

Above all, we are reminded to yield our child fully into God's hands in all things—there's no better place for him or her to be! That doesn't mean every choice your child makes as he or she grows up will be the right one. But when you place your little one's life—his or her *whole* life—into God's hands, then you'll know the peace that comes from trusting Him at all times, rather than the anxiety that comes from shouldering the full burden of parenting yourself.

Making It Happen—What are five ways you can pray right now for your child's future? Before the day ends, get together with your spouse and lift your child's future into the Lord's hands.

The Two Kinds of Fear

There is no fear in love. But perfect love drives out fear,
because fear has to do with punishment.
The one who fears is not made perfect in love.

(1 JOHN 4:18)

It's sad but true—some children are raised fearing their father. I don't mean in the sense we fear God—I mean *fear*. As in terrorized. As in a tender recruit under a no-nonsense Marine Corps Drill Instructor. And, sure enough, that kind of dread is one of the definitions of fear found in the dictionary, which says of this kind of fear, "to be afraid or apprehensive."

But Webster also offers another meaning for fear. In this definition, the word means "profound reverence and awe." It also notes that this fear is sometimes in reference to God.

Many men who had excellent fathers know this kind of fear can also apply to dads who know how to raise good kids. It's this second brand of paternal fear that's *good*. It offers a child security and tells the youngster that someone who knows the score is in charge. That when troubles come, this dad will *be there*. He will handle all the responsibilities for us—for we are weak and he is strong.

A strong dad is what kids need. A dad who wields his strength wisely—on behalf of his family, never as a weapon against it. This kind of man is feared in a way God Himself wishes to be feared.

If you have thought you must instill fear in your child, maybe it's because you were taught to fear your own dad. To continue this destructive cycle will only prevent the real bonding that takes place through genuine fatherly *affection*. A father who demands to be feared can't be truly affectionate. In the end he will be resented, either openly or inwardly. And he will never be feared with the reverence that satisfies the heart of both father and child.

If fear was part of your childhood and your father is still alive, you may have some issues you need to work out *soon*. If you were taught to fear with this kind of anxiety, your father may try to instill that same dread in your child. And just as bad, you—an adult man—may still be relating to your dad out of fear, distrust, anger, or some other negative emotion, rather than through the proper love of father and son.

The right kind of paternal fear is good. And you can build that godly fear in your child through tenderness and care—the same way God does for us.

Making It Happen—Consider these two kinds of fear. If the first one, the terrorizing fear, is what you felt toward your dad, make a date to talk with him. If it's just too hard, or if he's far away, write a letter. If he's no longer living, a letter can still be written—and then destroyed, after you've said what needs to be said. Then lift the matter to the Lord in prayer, asking for His wisdom and a forgiving heart.

Learn to cultivate the second kind of fear by using your emotional and physical strength to serve your family. Read Psalm 19 (slowly—it's a great read), which tells us that the fear of the Lord is *pure*, enduring forever.

Psalm 19

The heavens declare the glory of God;
    the skies proclaim the work of his hands.
Day after day they pour forth speech;
    night after night they display knowledge.
There is no speech or language
    where their voice is not heard.
Their voice goes out into all the earth,
    their words to the ends of the world.
In the heavens he has pitched a tent for the sun,
    which is like a bridegroom coming forth from his pavilion,
    like a champion rejoicing to run his course.
It rises at one end of the heavens and makes its circuit to the other;
    nothing is hidden from its heat.

The law of the Lord is perfect, reviving the soul.
The statutes of the Lord are trustworthy, making wise the simple.
The precepts of the Lord are right, giving joy to the heart.
The commands of the Lord are radiant, giving light to the eyes.
The fear of the Lord is pure, enduring forever.
The ordinances of the Lord are sure and altogether righteous.
They are more precious than gold,
    than much pure gold;
they are sweeter than honey,
    than honey from the comb.
By them is your servant warned;
    in keeping them there is great reward.

Who can discern his errors?
    Forgive my hidden faults.
Keep your servant also from willful sins;
    may they not rule over me.
Then will I be blameless,
    innocent of great transgression.
May the words of my mouth and the meditation of my heart
    be pleasing in your sight
    O Lord, my Rock and my Redeemer.

Bringing the World to Your Baby

God saw all that he had made,
and it was very good.

(GENESIS 1:31)

Imagine yourself in the shoes (or socks!) of a baby who is no more than six or eight months old. You're not able to walk yet. If you're really young, you're not even able to crawl. Much of the time, you're in a crib, playpen, or car seat. And each day, you find yourself looking at the same walls, the same room décor, the same mobile over the crib, and the same toys in the playpen. You hear pretty much the same noises around you day after day because your parents are settled into a fairly regular routine.

So when it comes to new sights, new sounds, and new experiences, you're at the mercy of your parents. You can't explore the fascinating world around you unless your parents go out of their way to change their routine, change what you're exposed to, and take you beyond your usual horizons.

That's why you squeal with delight or rivet your full attention when you see, feel, or hear a new sight, sensation, or sound. Of course, because you can't talk yet, you can't communicate your excitement to your parents. And when you've "been there, done that," you can't tell your folks you would like to see something new, something different.

Having taken a moment to see the world through babies' eyes, can you see how beneficial it is to broaden their world by *bringing* new experiences to them instead of leaving them to discover so much on their own when they get older?

Dad, how can you bring variety to your child's world?

- Don't make every toy available to him or her at any given time. Make some available, and keep others hidden away. Rotate the toys every few days and add a new one to the assortment every now and then.

- Come up with new baby games. Don't limit yourself to peek-a-boo and gentle tickling. Think of new ways to play with your hands together or to play with his or her limbs.

- Show your baby new objects. Make sure they are safe to touch and won't fit in the mouth.

- Show your child interesting pictures from different books. It's not important that he or she understand what the pictures are. The key is simply exposure to new sights.

- Vary your route when you go for a walk or ride. Don't take the same path around the neighborhood.

By bringing the world to your child, you'll broaden his or her horizons much more quickly and provide new mental and visual stimulation for growth. So if your daily routines have been the same for too long, do something different!

Making It Happen—What is one new sight, one new sound, and one new feel you can introduce to your child today?

The Bible Through a Dad's Eyes

Going a little farther, he fell to the ground and prayed that if possible the hour might pass from him. "Abba, Father," he said, "everything is possible for you. Take this cup from me. Yet not what I will, but what you will."

(MARK 14:35-36)

For you did not receive a spirit that makes you a slave again to fear, but you received the Spirit of sonship. And by him we cry, "Abba, Father." The Spirit himself testifies with our spirit that we are God's children.

(ROMANS 8:15-16)

Because you are sons, God sent the Spirit of his Son into our hearts, the Spirit who calls out, "Abba, Father."

(GALATIANS 4:6)

You may have been a reader of the Bible for a long time. But now that you're a dad, you'll begin to see some things you've never seen before. And some of the sermons you hear at church will make sense in a new way.

As we assume the identity of a father, a whole new world is opened to us—a new way of seeing. This is readily apparent as we read the Scriptures through new eyes. Verses that before seemed to hold only a limited meaning are now illuminated in a new way.

Consider the verses above. Although the Jews never referred to God using the Aramaic term *Abba,* Jesus chose this intimate word, which some scholars suggest might better be translated "daddy."

And it was in Jesus' darkest hour, as He prayed in the garden, that He used this endearing term when He asked His Father to let this cup pass from Him.

Abba is used twice more in the New Testament, as shown above. In both cases, the apostle Paul uses the term as a means of showing the reader the intimate relationship God has called His sons to. It's not just a cut-and-dried, "You're the son, I'm your Father" relationship being shown. Rather, it's the God of the universe who has chosen us to be His sons and Himself to be our Papa…our *tender* heavenly Father.

Reading this as a new father—and in the years to come—will give you an entirely new slant on your relationship to God as your "Dad."

You'll find the whole Bible is chock-full of messages that will be opened to you in a new fresh way…now that you're a dad.

Making It Happen—Although the Bible—and particularly the New Testament—does offer advice to dads, the greater rewards for you may be in the many verses that remind us of God's way of being a Father and "Abba Daddy" to us.

Here's an example…and a great verse to memorize:

> Which of you, if his son asks for bread, will give him a stone? Or if he asks for a fish, will give him a snake? If you, then, though you are evil, know how to give good gifts to your children, how much more will your Father in heaven give good gifts to those who ask him! So in every-thing, do to others what you would have them do to you, for this sums up the Law and the Prophets (Matthew 7:9-12).

What Does It Mean?

This is a day you are to commemorate;
for the generations to come you shall celebrate it
as a festival to the LORD—a lasting ordinance.

(EXODUS 12:14)

In Jewish families, it was dad's duty to teach the children what they needed to know. He was responsible for telling them the great story of the Exodus—God leading His people out of bondage. He also taught them the importance of God's law and the child's responsibility to it. And, of course, the story of the Passover was of utmost importance. At the Passover meal, a child would ask, "What does this mean?" and dad would tell the story of the first Passover and why it was important.

Dad, there's a lesson for us here. The primary responsibility for the child's spiritual and academic education is with *you.* In today's culture, such a notion seems backward, even (gasp!) sexist. But God isn't concerned with the fickle opinions of society. He has ordained the family as the means of bringing up children and has designated certain responsibilities to each parent. Mom will certainly teach the children also, whether you eventually choose to homeschool your child or educate him or her in a more traditional way.

Similarly, your child's spiritual growth isn't the responsibility of your church's Sunday school. They may certainly play a part, but it's your duty to answer the question, What does this mean? about so very many things your child will ask.

If this seems daunting…rest easy. God will show you how. Your wife will help—she has her part to play too—and so will the church. Believe me, it's doable. And not only doable…but also enjoyable.

Making It Happen—The days will come when your child will ask, What does this mean? in a variety of ways. It might be "How was I born?" Or "Is there really a God?" Or "What's on the other side of the universe?" But perhaps the most important question you can ever answer a child is…"Daddy, how did you become a Christian?"

Take a minute and think through how you'll answer. Were you raised in a Christian home? Who led you to Christ? Did you believe in Him right away, or did you take some convincing? Your personal stories about growing up and being a boy will be of great interest to your children. Don't hesitate to answer when they ask, "What does this mean?"

Home Is Where Dad Is

Near the cross of Jesus stood his mother, his mother's sister,
Mary the wife of Clopas, and Mary Magdalene.
When Jesus saw his mother there, and the disciple whom
he loved standing nearby, he said to his mother, "Dear woman,
here is your son," and to the disciple, "Here is your mother."
From that time on, this disciple took her into his home.

(JOHN 19:25-27)

Until I read this verse, I never really thought much about the disciples having a home—or what it might be like. But Jesus, in the last few minutes of His life, showed compassion for His earthly mother by commending her to His beloved disciple to become part of his family. To live in his *home*.

Home. Isn't it a great word? A home is a refuge, a haven, a *sanctuary*. Pity the person, child or adult, who hasn't a good home. And a good home doesn't just happen. It's not just a dorm with cafeteria service. It's not something created simply by some related people living in the same house.

A family home is made when a man and woman give up their independence to become interdependent with one another. They graft themselves together like a fine fruit tree with the firm intent that nothing will cause the home to splinter. In that irrevocable commitment called marriage, they set about building their *home* with purpose and resolve.

We often think of moms as the nest builders, but dads play a big part in creating a home, too. Most men, in fact, like to build, to fashion something lasting—most of us seem to have some innate desire to create. We might build a literal building or a business. We might create a novel or a painting.

But by far, the most important creative calling we men have in life is to build a home. A home with kids and laughter, banged-up knees, water balloon fights on a summer night, and popcorn gobbled in front of a favorite family video. A home filled with goodnight kisses and family prayer time. A home lavished in love and steeped in faith in the God who, one day many years ago, decided that the word *home* not only sounded nice, but was in itself a very good thing. So good that the Son of God, in His dying moments, made sure His mother had a home to go to.

When you think about it, building a home is like any other creative project. It requires vision, planning, time, imagination (lots of imagination!), hard work, the help of others, and lots of other special, often unexpected tasks. And as with most building projects, there will be mistakes, "back to the drawing board" days, frustrations—yes, they're all part of the creative process.

And just like any successful creative endeavor, our home-building mission comes with blueprints and the necessary tools to get the job done. The blueprints are unmistakably given in the Bible, where we read God's instructions for successful families—and we read of the shabby results in families where the blueprints were not followed (almost always due to dad's departure from the plan). The tools are plentiful: First and vastly underestimated is your own paternal instinct, implanted by God in every man, though many may have to unearth this often-buried instinct. Other tools for a successful family are the words of your mouth, the touch of your hand, and the sweat of your brow.

Look around you. You've got a job to do for the rest of your life. You're the general contractor for the building of a home. And like the expert craftsman, you'll want the finished product to be the *best*. Aim high, then, as you build your home. Let God give you a faith-picture for a home that's all the things it should be. And in this day of homelessness, your home can be a model for others to see. It can be a haven, a refuge, a sanctuary.

Dad, you're a master builder. With God's help and His blueprint in hand, you can build a successful family with your name on it and your leadership directing it. Go for it.

Build on, dad. And have a blessed home life.

Making It Happen—Think about the things that you see lacking in your home. Things that you and your wife can work on to make it more family-friendly. Write down three areas that need change or improvement, and then write something you can do to make that home improvement. Think of it in the same way you might visualize the changes you'd make in a remodel of your house.

1.

2.

3.

Let's end on an up note. List three things in your home that you can be proud of. What are you and your wife doing that you can say, as you would of a building project just completed, "Man, this is *good*"?

1.

2.

3.

Helping Your Baby Fall Asleep…
and Stay Asleep

Before I lay me down to sleep,
I thank You, gracious Lord,
for all Your kindness rich and deep,
and for Your loving words.

(A Traditional Prayer)

One of the blessings of newborns is that they sleep a lot. But newborns also grow quickly, and before you know it, your baby will become a bundle of perpetual energy! Getting a baby to fall asleep is one of the more creative challenges of parenting—and with that in mind, here are some tips you should find helpful:

Avoid playing actively with your baby just before bedtime. During the hour or two before you put your child to bed, create a quieter environment in the home that will help lull him or her toward sleep. Also, don't let your baby sleep more than a couple hours during late-afternoon naps or he or she will still be very much awake at bedtime.

It's normal for a baby to fuss for a few minutes before falling asleep. If your little one is making small noises, shuffling around a bit, or crying intermittently, leave your child for a few minutes to see if he or she falls asleep. Don't pick up your baby at the first sniffle, or you'll train him or her to think he or she can get your attention in a moment's notice. If your baby cries, wait for a brief time to see if he or she is lulled toward sleep. But if the little one is bawling away, then pick up and try to calm your baby. A baby is more likely to fall asleep when he or she has been calmed than while screaming.

When you go into a sleeping child's room, don't turn on the light, don't move the child (unless he or she is sleeping in an awkward position), and get out quickly. If the baby wakes up to be fed or changed, take care of matters in the dark. That might help baby go back to sleep faster. However, if you feed your child, you'll need to burp your little one and then try to cajole him or her to sleep in your arms.

And what if your child wails and just won't go to sleep? Have whoever is holding the baby give him or her to the other parent. For some reason, sometimes a mere change like this will help calm a child. If you're both tired, take turns so that one of you can rest. This will help prevent both of you from becoming equally frustrated and angry...which, for obvious reasons, is not a good situation.

Ultimately, the key to encouraging a baby toward healthy sleep patterns is to try different strategies and make note of the ones that work. Once you and your wife know what seems most effective for your baby, you will be able to develop a regular routine that helps make bedtime a more restful and enjoyable event for all of you.

Making It Happen—Find a bedtime routine that works, and stick with it. One especially helpful device for lulling your baby to sleep is a wind-up mechanical swing. Rocking your child in your arms can be effective, too. If there are certain toys or sounds that help your baby fall asleep, make sure to take those toys or sounds with you when you travel. Talk with your wife about ways you can create a consistent and comfortable environment for your baby's bedtimes.

Called by Name

He who has an ear, let him hear what the Spirit says to the churches. To him who overcomes, I will give some of the hidden manna. I will also give him a white stone with a new name written on it, known only to him who receives it.

(Revelation 2:17)

One distant day from now, we will each be given a new name, one chosen especially for us by our heavenly Father. In the meantime, we will be known by the name chosen by our earthly parents.

There's a lot of importance in a name. A son named after dad will have a legacy, either good or bad, attached to it. Your family's last name has some importance, too. Your new baby is the most recent in a long line of Smiths, or Joneses, or whoevers. He or she thus has a heritage. And your child's identity can be influenced by understanding his or her place in that long family line. It's not necessary to join a genealogical society or to trace your ancestors back several generations. What you already know about your heritage right now will give you a good start.

Children can learn that they are a part of something larger than themselves—part of a family that has gone on before. Part of a tradition. As they grow, and as you begin to offer bedtime stories or conversation at mealtimes, tell your children from where they come. Instill in your children a sense of family history—not just yours, but also your wife's. Let them know that they have a family name to live up to. Make sure they understand that their ancestors of yesteryear (if they could speak) would look to your children to proudly bear the family name with honor. They would urge your children to never, *never* do anything that would bring dishonor on the family name.

Songwriter Steve Chapman's powerful song "Remember Whose Child You Are" is a favorite of mine. It reminds me that not only do I bear the earthly name of some rugged and honorable ancestors in whose honorable shadows I walk, but I also bear the name and image of a heavenly Father to whom I must also be accountable for the family name of "Christian."

Making It Happen—If you've never before considered your family heritage, do so now. Find out from living relatives some of the stories of honor and heroics that are in your family line. Write them down or record them on videotape so your children will have a record of their earthly heritage.

This will help form your children's identity, and it will help instill a sense of duty…of obligation to those who have gone on before to "remember whose children they are."

Your local library or bookstore has books with the definitions of names. Find out what your son or daughter's name means and, if you're at all handy, make a plaque with the child's name and its meaning and hang it in a prominent place.

Growing Stronger Under Pressure

I can do everything through him who gives me strength.

(PHILIPPIANS 4:13)

Have you had one of those days when you can't seem to do anything right? The tape on a brand-new disposable diaper tears off as you change the baby, forcing you to start all over again. You warm the milk bottle too long, and it needs time to cool off—while a very loud and hungry baby gets even louder and hungrier. As you burp your little one, the burp just won't come...then all of a sudden, Mt. Vesuvius! And no burp cloth in sight. As you set up the playpen, your thumb is wickedly pinched by the frame, and now your thumbnail is several shades of red and purple. And through it all, the baby keeps crying and crying—with no "off" switch available so you can bring relief to your headache.

I had days—plenty of them—when everything went wrong. By the end of the day, I would gripe to God that I just wasn't cut out for fatherhood and that my wife, Becky, would have to raise the kids. I figured if I couldn't do anything right, it was better not to do anything at all.

But as I sulked through the next day or two, I would come to realize my attitude wasn't right, nor was resignation the answer. And as I "grew up" in my role as a father, I began to see that when it came to dealing with the pressures of fatherhood, I had two choices: I could let the pressure mold me into a better father, or I could crumble.

Let's look at two ways we can respond to pressure that will make us stronger and more resilient as fathers:

Let pressure drive you toward God, not away from Him. When problems arise, all too often we say, "I can't do it. I give up. It's impossible." But problems give us the perfect opportunity to go to the One who is stronger, wiser, and more capable than we are. Philippians 4:13 says it perfectly: "I can do everything through him who gives me strength." With God's help, you can do *everything*—and that includes fulfilling your calling as a father. If you succumb to pity parties the way I did, you'll only stew in your frustration and get nowhere. But if you go to God, you'll feel a renewed sense of strength…and resume making progress in the right direction. The progress might be slow at times, but it will be sure.

Let pressure drive you to your knees in prayer. When we prayerfully surrender our problems to the Lord, our worries will be replaced by peace. "Do not be anxious for anything…present your requests to God. And the peace of God, which transcends all understanding, will guard your hearts and your minds" (Philippians 4:6-7). That may seem rather simple, but it really does work. It's God's promise to you.

Yes, you will continue to have those occasional bad days. But just because the world around you is falling apart doesn't mean you have to fall apart. When the pressure comes, go to God and pour your heart out to Him. He's ready to listen…and to help.

Making It Happen—Write Philippians 4:13 and Philippians 4:6-7 on a 3 x 5 index card. Carry the card around with you for the next several days until you memorize the verses. Then when pressure comes your way, you can call upon these two promises from God and act upon them.

Together Forever

Are you married? Do not seek a divorce.

(1 Corinthians 7:27)

I know—it seems so impossible. You and your wife are no doubt very happy and enjoying your family life. But the best time to reflect on divorce is now, while it's not an issue. And making the decision to stay together *for better or worse* is the best thing you can do for your new baby.

In an article in *Marriage Partnership* magazine pollster George Barna noted that the divorce rate among born-again Christians was at 27 percent and 30 percent for fundamentalist Christians.[9] This is actually *higher* than the rate for non-Christians—which is 23 percent. Interestingly, the surveyors were careful to ask the respondents if they had been divorced before or after they became Christians, and 87 percent said "after."

Dads, that means that it's likely that one in four of you reading this book will eventually split from your wife—and your children. That must not be. Not only for your children's sake... but also for yours.

A recent study by the Institute in American Values showed that most divorces were highly preventable and that most who divorced later regretted it. The research showed that only half of those who divorced were any happier five years after their divorce, while two-thirds of those worked through their marital problems eventually found happiness in their troubled marriage. Even those who divorced and remarried were less happy than those who had endured the tough times in their marriage.

In reference to his survey, George Barna noted, "A person's faith doesn't seem to have a lot of effect on whether they'll get divorced. Even among born-again Christians, most don't exhibit attitudes or behaviors any different than non-Christians."

Whoa! How then are we Christians if we don't have a different attitude or behavior than non-Christians? How does our faith in Christ affect our lives if not in the very basic way it influences how we relate to our wives and children?

So what's the solution?

You and your wife can actually *decide* that you will never divorce. You can covenant together to work through any serious difficulty that threatens your home. And you can stay active in a good strong church fellowship that supports strong marriages. Having an enduring marriage, guys, isn't simply the luck of the draw. It's based on two people agreeing to be partners for life...no matter what.

Making It Happen—Why not talk to your wife tonight about the above statistics. Reaffirm to each other your commitment to work through the inevitable patchy spots ahead (all marriages have them—but not all marriages end because of them).

Decide together to remove the word *divorce* from your vocabulary. This is God's word for you: "Are you married? Do not seek a divorce."

Remembering Dad

A father to the fatherless...

(PSALM 68:5)

What was your dad like? Was he a Christian? A lover of his children? Was he there for you when you needed him? Was he consumed with anger? Aloof? Did he drink too much? Was he a hypocrite? A scoundrel? A saint? Superdad?

We dads enter fatherhood with some baggage—both good and bad. Every one of us had a dad of our own—at least biologically, if not relationally. Maybe he was a total flake who simply impregnated your mom and left. Or maybe he was the pillar of the church—the most godly man you've ever known. In either case, you have certain ideas about what a father is and does based on your own experience.

Some new dads, in an effort to not repeat the same costly mistakes their dads made, find themselves making a whole new set of mistakes. If their dads were too harsh, they become too permissive. If their dads never encouraged them (in sports, for example), they may insist their own child participate in an activity which the child doesn't enjoy or for which he or she has no talent.

Other dads may simply perpetuate the mistakes their fathers made, since that was the only example of fatherhood they've seen. If they were abused, they may be abusers themselves. If their dads were distant and unaffectionate, they too may find offering affection to their child very difficult.

But there's a better way. You can overcome the influence of a negative role model. Sure, you can learn from the successes and failures of your own dad, but to be really effective, relax a bit and let God fashion you into a good dad. How does He do this? First, by being a faithful dad Himself. Watch how God fathers you. Then, He may also give you some good mentors—your own dad (if he was a good one), other dads at church, or other men whose fathering skills you admire. You may find God attracting you to some of the excellent Christian books on fathering, and you may want to attend (or maybe even facilitate) a dad's group at church. By making fatherhood a priority you'll ensure that you become a memorable dad to your own kids.

Making It Happen—Think about your earthly father. Pick three words that best describe him. Choose his best trait as a dad—and then his worst. Finally, think back to your grandfather. How might the mistakes he made while raising your dad have led to mistakes your dad may have made in your life? How might the goodness of your grandfather been evident in your dad's fathering skills?

Finally, if your father failed you…it's time to move on. Forgive him *fully* and turn to your own duties as a dad. Someday your own child may find something in you that will need forgiving.

The Drive Home

As God's chosen people, holy and dearly loved,
clothe yourselves with compassion, kindness,
humility, gentleness, and patience.

(Colossians 3:12)

What usually goes through your mind as you drive home from work?

Most likely you think about the day's events—what got accomplished, what didn't, conversations or meetings that took place, things other people did that pleased or discouraged you, and so on. During the drive home we can reflect, bring closure to the day, and consider our plan of action for tomorrow.

While it's valuable for us to bring closure to the day, there's a negative side effect we need to watch for. Sometimes we end up dragging our tiredness, foul mood, and stress home with us and let them affect our interaction with our wife and children. For whatever reason, we may end up snapping at a loved one or detaching ourselves from others. I know, because I've been there. I've unloaded negative workday baggage on my family—with undesirable results.

It was during one of my drives home that I felt convicted about this problem and wanted to bring about a change. That's when I came up with my "halfway point" idea.

This is how it works: When I am halfway home, I try to remember to push aside all thoughts of work and begin praying. I pray for myself—that I'll arrive home ready to love and interact with my wife and children. I pray that during those first few moments after I set foot in the door, I'll be a positive influence rather than a negative one. I pray for my wife to have a renewed strength as she prepares dinner and cares for the children. I pray that though I feel drained, I'll be refreshed with a second wind of energy so I can give my wife and children the kind of attention that says, "I love you." And I remind myself that I'm not able to do this in my own strength, and that I need the Lord's enablement to make it happen.

And you know what? It really works. Setting my mind to prayer and reminding myself I'm a husband and father has made a big difference in the way I act toward my family upon arriving at home.

Of course, I'm still learning. I don't always notice when I reach the halfway point. Sometimes I'm so preoccupied I miss that marker. But with time, I've gotten better, and the results have been great.

Making It Happen—Where is your halfway point? Figure out where it is, and begin your ministry of praying for your family (and your attitudes) before you arrive home. You might find it more effective to actually pull off the road a few blocks from home and, in prayerful silence, make that mental shift from being a worker to being a dad.

—⚙—

Go with the Flow

For you created my inmost being;
you knit me together in my mother's womb.

(PSALM 139:13)

Recently a parent asked Dr. James Dobson, founder of Focus on the Family, his observations about what were apparently inborn differences in his children. One, the dad noted, was strong willed from birth. Another child seemed to be quite compliant, also from birth. Dr. Dobson confirmed this dad's observation—some children have specific inborn temperamental differences.

This parent wasn't the first to notice that certain personality traits, which in the past have often been attributed soley to a child's home environment, are actually genetically transmitted, just like hair or eye color. Of course, the home will definitely influence how some of these inborn traits are developed. Will that strong-willed boy become a leader or a rebel? Will that compliant daughter be passive when she should take a stand? Will she allow people to take advantage of her?

Dad, part of your job is to notice the personality "bent" God has placed in your child. Accept that bent and try to find creative ways to direct that bent towards a positive outcome.

Think about your own personality. What aspects of your personality do you think may have been inborn? How did your parents help or hurt the development of your personality? Did they accept you as you are, with your inborn strengths and

———

163

weaknesses, affirming the former and helping you shore up the latter?

If not, you can no doubt see how important it will be for you to work *with* your child's temperament, not against it. Why paddle against the current? Why cut against the grain? Go with the flow of your child's temperament and watch him or her shine.

Making It Happen—Below are some character-istics that most parents might consider, well, a challenge. In parenthesis I've included Bible char-acters who might have exhibited these charac-teristics. How might these qualities be channeled into positive attributes?

- melancholy (Moses)

- strong willed (Paul)

- fearful (Peter)

- curious (Eve)

- stubborn (Jonah)

- insensitive (Martha)

Dads in the Bible, Part 1

*Everything that was written in the past was written
to teach us, so that through endurance and the encouragement
of the Scriptures we might have hope.*

(Romans 15:4)

Have you ever noticed the number of dads in the Bible who made mistakes? We can find example after example of fathers who failed their children in one way or another. And while we certainly would not want to follow in their footsteps, there are valuable lessons we can learn from them. In fact, we can be certain God included their stories in the Bible for that very reason.

The danger of irresponsibility. When it came time for Abraham and Lot to choose a place to live, Lot "pitched his tent near Sodom. Now the men of Sodom were wicked and were sinning greatly against the Lord" (Genesis 13:12-13). Why did Lot choose to settle his wife and daughters in an evil city? We don't know, but it's clear Lot wasn't thinking about the well-being of his family. As dads, we bear the responsibility of protecting and preserving our family from worldly influences.

The danger of favoritism. Jacob had 12 sons. He made it obvious he favored Joseph over all the others, giving him a beautiful many-colored tunic. This provoked the other brothers to jealousy, and they came to hate Joseph (Genesis 37:3-4). We as dads need to love and treat all our children equally.

The danger of neglect. Eli was the high priest at the tabernacle at Shiloh, some 20 miles north of Jerusalem. His sons were also priests, but they "were wicked men; they had no regard for the

LORD" (1 Samuel 2:12). They abused the sacrificial offerings and slept with the women who served at the tabernacle. Evidently Eli didn't put much effort into correcting the situation, for God said to him, "Why do you...honor your sons more than me?" (verse 29). Eli's neglect allowed the mockery of God, the sacrificial system, and the people of Israel to continue unchecked (verse 35).

The danger of sexual compromise. David's unbridled lust for Bathsheba—who belonged to another man—led to a pregnancy out of wedlock and the killing of Bathsheba's husband in an effort to hide the sin. What's mind-boggling is that it all started with a simple *look*. David took just *one* step on the road to sexual compromise, and the rest was a blur. Did David's lack of restraint have anything to do with the fact his sons Amnon and Absalom lacked sexual restraint as well? We can't help but wonder. Whatever the case, we as dads can't afford to allow a first step that becomes a rapid descent down the slope of immorality.

We could consider more accounts like the ones above, but we've looked at enough to know this: Our actions (or lack of them) can often affect how our children turn out. In all that we do as dads, then, may we have a zeal for our children's long-term welfare that helps us reject the lure of any short-term indulgences that may derail us...and our families.

Making It Happen—Let's think of how we can avoid the traps Lot, Jacob, Eli, and David fell into. What could Lot have done differently for his family? How could Jacob have prevented jealousy from arising? How could Eli have remedied the problems with his sons? What should David have done when he saw Bathsheba? Challenging ourselves with questions like these will help us to build our discernment and make better decisions.

Dads in the Bible, Part 2

*Everything that was written in the past was written
to teach us, so that through endurance and the encouragement
of the Scriptures we might have hope.*

(ROMANS 15:4)

For the last several years of his baseball career, Brett Butler played for the Los Angeles Dodgers. He was a classic example of an all-around, multitalented player. He was someone who could be counted on to get results for his team—both offensively and defensively. He was so consistently good in many different areas that he was often asked, "What's your secret?" He said, in essence, "Each year I pick a ballplayer who is one of the best at a skill I want to master. Then I spend the whole season trying to be as good as him in that skill." Because Brett picked a different player each year, he was always developing different abilities. And though he was already an excellent player himself, he recognized that it's always beneficial to have role models who can help you build your skills.

With that in mind, let's look at some role-model fathers in the Bible and see what qualities we can learn from them:

Noah, a man of persistence. Noah spent 120 years building the ark (Genesis 6:3,14). Many Bible scholars believe it had never rained upon the earth up to this time. It was definitely an act of faith when Noah continued to build the ark for 120 years without understanding how God would flood the earth. When it comes to God's promises, many of us give up after waiting a few days, weeks, or at most, months. But 120 years? That's persistence—and as we know, it paid off.

Zacharias, a man of commitment. Zacharias, an elderly priest, and his wife, Elizabeth, "were both righteous before God.... But they had no child...and they were both well advanced in years" (Luke 1:6-7 NKJV). One day an angel announced to Zacharias that he and Elizabeth would have a child (John the Baptist). Apparently Zacharias had been "righteous" all through his years as a priest—not an easy accomplishment, considering many of his fellow and superior priests were corrupt. He remained committed to serving God uprightly in spite of the negative influences around him.

Joseph, a man of bold initiative. After the wise men arrived in Bethlehem to worship the child Jesus, an angel appeared and told Joseph, "Get up...take the child and his mother and escape to Egypt.... for Herod is going to search for the child to kill him" (Matthew 2:13). Joseph departed immediately for this long and difficult journey, not knowing where he would find shelter or how he would support his family in this strange and faraway land. In fear and uncertainty he could have resisted God's command, but he didn't. He boldly took the initiative to do what was necessary to protect his family.

What made Noah, Zacharias, and Joseph special as fathers? Scripture makes it evident all three walked in a close relationship with their heavenly Father. And just as it made a difference in their lives, it can make a difference in yours, too—helping you to be persistent, committed, and bold.

Making It Happen—Just as Brett Butler learned from other ballplayers, you can learn from other Christian fathers. Is there a skill you've observed in another dad that you would like to develop in yourself? Specify the skill you want to learn, observe that dad, and cultivate that skill in your own life.

A Safety Checklist for Your Home

A prudent man sees danger and takes refuge,
but the simple keep going and suffer for it.

(PROVERBS 22:3)

A curious child sees something worth investigating and off he or she goes, usually oblivious to possible dangers. We all know the tragic stories of small children dashing into the path of a car, accidentally drinking toxic fluids within easy reach under the sink, or wandering away into an unenclosed swimming pool.

Although these tragedies usually involve toddlers, not infants, now is the time for you to carefully inspect the house for dangers that might present problems in a few months. Your son or daughter will soon be wobbling along on his or her new legs and, even sooner, crawling toward existing dangers.

When you think about it, this world is full of dangers for us adults, and God, through His Word, has instructed us to stay away from danger. The book of Proverbs is a must for any man. For example, we're warned to stay far away from indulging in strong wine, toying with sexual immorality, and leaning on our own fleshly wisdom.

The day will come for you to instruct your child in the dangers he or she will face outside of your home: drugs, peer pressure, and a worldly value system that is increasingly anti-God. But for now, you can take some simple steps toward making your home as safe as possible.

Making It Happen—Here are some ideas:

1. Buy electrical outlet covers that will keep a little one from sticking things into sockets.

2. Make sure any pools of water—fountains, swimming pools, even birdbaths—are not left uncovered. If there's no fence between your yard and a neighboring pool, build one.

3. Fix or replace any furniture that can easily topple over. A crawling baby, learning to pull himself up on his legs, will look for a prop to pull himself up.

4. Remove all poisons from under the sink and keep them on a high shelf in the utility room or garage.

5. Look for anything that might break into sharp pieces that could cut your baby. Move all such breakables to higher shelves.

6. Make sure your car is safe too. Install an age-approved baby seat and use it at all times. Persuade mom not to succumb to the temptation to nurse the baby as you travel. If nursing is necessary, pull over to a rest stop. A baby's neck can be easily snapped by the force of a deployed air bag.

7. When visiting, glance around for possible dangers. Make sure any relatives' houses where the baby will frequently visit are also safe.

Winning Our Children

Train a child in the way he should go,
and when he is old he will not turn from it.

(Proverbs 22:6)

One of the worst tragedies facing the church in modern times is the loss of our children's faith as they mature into adults. Parents are both caregivers to their children and missionaries. In fact, your children are your primary mission field. And yet so many parents fail in this one most important task. Think about some of the parents you know whose children are now adults. Consider how many of them constantly seek prayer for their wayward children.

The loss of our children to the enemy is a disgrace. We are given stewardship over the children God has entrusted to us. How then can we be such weak parents as to allow them to be siphoned off from the faith?

You are now at the start of your child's life. But what will his or her life be like 20 years from now? Will he or she too be lost, searching for the meaning in life they should have known all along, by trying drugs, sexual immorality, or the vogue philosophy of the day?

And what about you? Where will you be in 20 years? Pleading with your church for prayers for your lost child? You have the opportunity *now* to do what you can to prevent that from happening.

Making It Happen—Here are some tips (and some blanks for you to add a few yourself):

1. Live your faith before your child. Let him or her see the gospel worked out in your life.

2. Be faithful to the church where God has planted your family.

3. Watch out for temptations to earn more money at the expense of your family life.

4. Learn to be a *giver:* not just financially, but of yourself—your time, your praise, and your affection.

5. Lovingly discipline your child, insisting he or she learns right from wrong at an early age.

6. Be at peace with your wife.

7. Involve the family in some sort of ministry, even if it's as simple as helping support a child in a foreign land.

8. Pray confidently for your children daily.

9. Have a regular time when you read God's Word to them and pray with them.

10. Develop small personal rituals of love that are individual to each child and exist as a semisecret between you.

11. Eat meals together.

12. Acquaint your little one with the great heroes of the faith. By the time every child has become an adult he or she should know

———

such names as Corrie ten Boom, Jim Elliot, Amy Carmichael, George Mueller, and many others. There are some fine books that tell the stories of these warriors of the faith. Hold these role models up as examples worthy of emulation.

13. Shield your children from evil. They, like you, are to know of evil from a distance, *not* experientially.

14. Be a man of your word. Don't make promises you won't keep.

15. _____
    _____.

16. _____
    _____.

17. _____
    _____.

18. _____
    _____.

Do these things, and your child is far less likely to end up a casualty on the field of spiritual battle.

Prayer and Family Planning

Sons are a heritage from the LORD,
children a reward from him.
Like arrows in the hands of a warrior
are sons born in one's youth.
Blessed is the man whose quiver is full of them.
They will not be put to shame
when they contend with their enemies in the gate.

(PSALM 127:3-5)

Have you and your wife decided just how full your quiver will be? Many couples are faithful Christians: They attend a good church, they're involved with other couples in ministry, they give freely of their finances, and they pray, of course. But how earnestly do they pray about the size of their family? Do they simply decide how many children to have according to personal preference, convenience, or budgetary reasoning?

God has never rescinded His command to be fruitful and multiply. He will bless you with as many children as you'll make room for. The operative word is *bless.* While the world considers children a burden to be "planned" or aborted if inconvenient, God's idea of babies is much easier and more positive: They're a *blessing!* The psalmist wrote that a man with a quiver full of children was *blessed,* not burdened.

In a day when many are refusing the blessings of children, it's rare to find Christians who have decided the size of their family by carefully praying about it and then leaving God room to amend their plan. One brave and godly couple I know decided to have dad's vasectomy reversed after they were convinced they had usurped a decision that was ultimately God's, not theirs. As it turned out, they had no more children, but their decision left that choice up to God.

Dad, a large family is a lot of work and expense. But I've never met a father of several children who regretted the life of any one of his kids.

As you pray about this very important decision, there are really only two practical considerations:

1. Most of the work in a large family falls to mom as she maintains the house and home. Has God gifted her with the desire (and energy) to care for several children?

2. How about you? Will you be on the scene enough to provide leadership for a good-sized family?

You notice I didn't include money as a consideration. God calls *every* Christian to live by faith in *every* area. In the nineteenth century, George Mueller and his wife founded an orphanage that eventually spilled over to five houses, and they were vital in the raising of some 2000 boys and girls. Although he knew he was called to this special ministry, he still had to feed every one of these children—by faith. Many were the days when he literally didn't know where the next meal would come from—but God never failed to provide.

Whether you're called to be a father of only one child or many, you will still need to rely on God to provide through you. Never limit the size of your family without putting the matter confidently before God. He will guide.

Making It Happen—Discuss with your wife the importance of prayer and trusting in God in determining the size of your family. Pray *together* about this.

Unfinished Business

Be very careful, then, how you live—not as unwise but as wise,
making the most of every opportunity...

(EPHESIANS 5:15-16)

Life is fragile.

Just last month, a dear friend of ours died much too young. Pam was always filled to overflowing with enthusiasm and energy. You could count on her to give 200 percent of herself to anything she did. She was passionate about her family, her ministry of interpreting for the deaf, her Sunday school class-room full of children. She didn't do things halfheartedly. She dove in with both hands, both feet, and all her heart. If anyone could have outlasted the Energizer bunny, it was Pam.

But a few months ago, we heard through a mutual friend that she had been hit hard with an aggressive form of cancer. And in much too short a time, she was gone...leaving two teen children whom we're sure will make a difference in the lives of others because she took the time to make a difference in them.

My wife, Becky, and I know of several children in our church who lost a mom or dad while still at a very tender age. You can be certain none of those now-deceased parents would have planned it that way. All of them would have wanted to see their children grow up, start a career, get married, and have children of their own. None of us include "premature death" as a part of our immediate plans. We prefer to think of it as something that happens to someone else. But the truth is, we just never know.

I know two pastors who, on their desks, have a framed picture of a family tombstone in a cemetery. Both have their picture prominently displayed for the same reason: They want a constant reminder that helps them keep all of life in perspective. What's really important? I could die at any time. If I were to do so, would I have any unfinished business here on planet Earth?

What about you? Is there something you're putting off till tomorrow that you need to do today with your little one? With your wife? With someone else? In the rush to keep up with the demands of life, I've found it all too easy to put off an evening of fun and meaningful interaction with my sons. I've let too much time go by since the last time I told each of them, "I love you and care about you." I've let the material and replaceable things of life stand in the way of the irreplaceable. And too many times, I've found myself thinking, *Lord, I sure hope I'm not called home now, because I have some unfinished business with my children...my wife...a family member...a friend.*

But...you just never know. As I said earlier, life is fragile. So if you can make it happen today, then make it happen today. As dads, let's live in such a way that unfinished business is not one of our concerns. It will mean a lot to your loved ones.

Making It Happen—You're young, you're in reasonably good health, and your future stretches before you like a long road into the far horizon, right? Our hope is that God will grant you many years of life and happiness. Yet if something should happen to you—should you become disabled, suffer from a prolonged illness, or die—what will become of your family? Have you prayerfully laid out a plan for the security of those you love?

Here are some essential basics:

1. Budget some savings from every paycheck. Either invest it or put it in a joint account with both your name and your wife's name on it.

2. Ask your pastor, dad, or a trusted friend to recommend a good insurance agent. Together with your wife, meet this agent to discuss your options. Ask questions. Weigh your choices and decide together how much insurance coverage you need.

3. Don't mount up a pile of bills. Keep only one credit card and pay off the balance every month so interest charges don't erode your finances.

4. If at all possible, pay over and above what's necessary to pay on your home mortgage payments. One additional payment a year or an extra $25 or $50 a month can whittle time off your mortgage quickly.

5. Ask around for recommendations for a good lawyer. Have him write wills for both you and your wife. Specify who should raise your child in the event both you and your spouse die together. Of course, you two will need to talk this over with the person whom you name as guardian and get his or her consent for this.

6. Commit your plans to God, and rest easy—you've done a good thing by planning for emergencies.

The Spirit of the Home

Extol the LORD, O Jerusalem;
praise your God, O Zion,
for he strengthens the bars of your gates
and blesses your people within you.
He grants peace to your borders
and satisfies you with the finest of wheat.

(PSALM 147:12-14)

Have you ever walked into a house and immediately sensed the peace of God? Some homes are like that. Unfortunately, in other homes there seems to be an air of discord or strife...you just sense it. Maybe it's because you know the people who live there lack the peace of God.

But for the Christian, the home is a small representation of what heaven must be like. Christ, after all, lives in the home of the Christian family. As the saying goes:

> Christ is the Head of this house
> The Unseen Guest at every meal
> The Silent Listener in every conversation

Both father and mother must partner together to ensure their home is a Christian home—not just in name but in practice and in spirit. Such a godly home will be like a light to families who are searching for peace and security.

For if Christ is *not* present in the home, the family is open to the powerful influence of the enemy of home life—Satan. As the great Bible teacher of the past Matthew Henry said, "If you have not a church in your house, it is to be feared Satan will have a seat there. If religion does not rule in your families, sin and wickedness will rule there."

Perhaps no greater illustration of this can be offered than the famous nineteenth-century study of the Edwards and Jukes families.

Max Jukes was not a believer in Christ. He gave his life to drinking and immorality. When his children asked to go to church, he refused them. The Jukes home was devoid of any Christian life whatsoever. The result, according to this seven-year study, was that Max Jukes left a legacy of approximately 1000 descendants over the course of the next century or more, including 130 convicts, 27 murderers, 190 prostitutes, and more than 500 alcoholics or drug addicts. Many others simply became paupers, dependent on the state of New York to provide for them.

In contrast, the family of the great Christian preacher and family patriarch Jonathan Edwards also produced approximately 1000 descendants in the same time period, including more than 300 ministers, 75 authors, 86 college professors, 13 university presidents, 7 Congressmen, 3 governors, and 1 vice president of the United States.

In one of his sermons, Edwards said, "Every family ought to be a little church, consecrated to Christ and wholly influenced and governed by His rules. And family education and order are some of the chief means of grace. If these fail, all other means are like to prove ineffectual."

Yes, every household will have a legacy. You and your wife will help determine what kind of lives your descendants will live. You have a hand in the outcome of all who follow your blood-line.

So make no mistake about it—a home *will* reflect the mood of its inhabitants. It *will* impact future generations. There's nothing spooky or mystical about it. A family filled with strife will have a home with a strifeful spirit. And a home where God is honored and His order is in place—where dad is respected and respectful of his family—will know abundant peace and leave a wonderful legacy for the next generation.

Making It Happen—In addition to being a godly dad, there are some other important ways you can establish a positive spirit in your home:

1. Teach your children to be kind toward one another and respectful toward adults. Teach them good manners and cultivate a calm spirit in them.

2. Communicate positively with your wife—don't argue.

3. Make prayer and the reading of God's Word a common practice.

4. Carefully consider what TV shows your family watches. Avoid programs that assault the values of family life, depict immorality, or promote profane language and living.

5. Listen to music that is joyful and uplifting, not frenetic and full of discord.

6. Keep the house reasonably orderly. It doesn't have to look like the setting for a photo shoot for *Good Housekeeping*...but it needs to reflect cleanliness and order.

7. Read good books to the family regularly.

8. Welcome friends into your home. The peaceful home is a wonderful witnessing tool, testifying to what the presence of God in a home can mean.

---

9. Live within the family budget. You can avoid much family strife by spending money wisely.

10. Play together. Regular fun times are a natural part of a joyful family. Make sure laughter is common and tears are scarce.

Does this sound like the kind of home you'd like to have? It *can* be yours to a surprising degree. Not all the time, and not in every area...but you can begin making some positive changes today.

Daring to Discipline

Endure hardship as discipline; God is treating you as sons.
For what son is not disciplined by his father? If you are not
disciplined (and everyone undergoes discipline), then you are
illegitimate children and not true sons. Moreover,
we have all had human fathers who disciplined us
and we respected them for it.

(HEBREWS 12:7-9)

Effective fathers learn how to discipline a disobedient child. Love and discipline are the two hands of fatherhood. One hand acknowledges the deep bond between a father and child, the kind of bond that hates to see pain in the beloved. The other hand knows full well that left untrained, the twig will indeed grow crooked. Love weeps as it inflicts the temporary pain of chastisement, but it cries for joy when it tastes the sweet and lasting fruit of obedience.

Mark these words: a child who is *appropriately* disciplined will be a happy, well-adjusted, and *grateful* adult. An untrained child will become the slave of his or her passions and desires as an adult. A child who does not learn self-control will certainly lack it in adulthood.

So when and how does discipline start? It starts *only* when the child displays willful disobedience. Accidents are not worthy of punishment—only disobedience is. The earliest implementation of fatherly discipline is simply the firm verbal reprimand, "No," when the child has learned what "no" means. For new dads, that day is in the considerable future. *No child under the age of 18 months should be physically punished by any means.*

Now is the time to read the book suggested below. The day will come soon enough when your verbal "no" will be tested as the child continues his or her willful disobedience. At that time, dad can begin finding the appropriate punishment for this particular child.

Physical abuse is a horrible problem in our society. Loving discipline bears no resemblance to it whatsoever. In fact, the wholesale abandonment of corporeal punishment is itself a terrible form of abuse. Each childhood age has a different way in which this correction should be administered. A child must never be struck so as to leave marks. Nor should babies ever be shaken or touched roughly. Never. *Never.* Just as a tree that is properly staked will likely grow straight and tall, a child who is loving and carefully disciplined is much more likely to walk straight on the path of life and bring joy to his or her parents' hearts.

Making It Happen—One of the classic Christian books on this subject is Dr. James Dobson's *The New Dare to Discipline.* Pick it up at almost any bookstore…it's been around for a long time and has sold more than 3.5 million copies. Then, bookmark the website for Dr. Dobson's Focus on the Family (www.family.org). This is a site you'll want to visit often—there's a lot of good advice there, and Dr. Dobson, a pediatrician by trade, is a dad's best friend.

Training *Yourself* in the Way You Should Go

Follow my example, as I follow the example of Christ.

(1 CORINTHIANS 11:1)

In the book of Proverbs, the "wisdom book" of the Bible, is tucked away one of the most powerful principles God has given us about parenting: "Train a child in the way he should go, and when he is old he will not turn from it" (22:6). The point of this proverb is that it's important to teach our children all that is good and right, and reinforce those principles time and again so they will walk the right path in life.

There's a variation of that proverb I would encourage you to remember while your child is still a baby: Train *yourself* in the way you should go so that your child won't catch you departing from it. No, you won't find that proverb in the Bible, but speaking from personal experience, I can assure you that you will want to abide by it. As your child grows older, you're going to notice a rather interesting phenomenon.

Little children are quite lenient on themselves when it comes to breaking your rules. Though you may catch them doing wrong and warn them not to do it again, they are likely to do it again. And perhaps even again and again.

But if *you* happen to break a rule and your child notices it, believe me, you won't hear the end of it.

From the beginning, we've always had a rule in our house that the kids cannot take food or drinks into the living room unless they use a TV tray. After countless spills (and permanent stains that stand as silent witnesses to our children's disobedience), we still find ourselves telling our kids (now teenagers) to use a TV tray when they snack in the living room.

But if one of us parents should happen to wander into the living room with a can of soda or a cookie in hand and the kids are around to witness the "crime," they literally shout with glee as they incriminate us for breaking our own rule. Sometimes they're so zealous you would think we had committed the unpardonable sin.

If you break a rule, you'll soon hear your children say, "If you can break the rules, then we can, too."

As parents, we may think it's unfair for children to be highly tolerant of hypocrisy within themselves yet display no tolerance at all toward their parents. But that's not the point. The best policy is this: Follow the same rules you give to your children. You might think that's unfair as well, but consider this: Consistency breeds respect. Your children will appreciate that you abide by the very expectations you place on them. By disciplining yourself in certain ways, you'll encourage discipline in their own lives. And when you're a model of consistency to your child, you'll find it much easier to train your children in the way they should go.

Making It Happen—Write 1 Corinthians 11:1 on a 3 x 5 index card and memorize it: "Follow my example, as I follow the example of Christ." The apostle Paul wasn't afraid to ask his fellow Christians to follow his example, just as he followed Christ's example. Commit yourself to being able to say these same words to your own children.

The Greatest Joy:
The Salvation of a Soul

In reply Jesus declared, "I tell you the truth,
no one can see the kingdom of God unless he is born again."

(JOHN 3:3)

Dad, when did you accept Christ into your life? For me, it was as a college student. My early childhood was filled with church, but somehow the good news of the gospel escaped me...until my heart was ready.

Since that day, years ago, I've seen many godly families with children who have come to know Christ at an early age. In some ways I envy those kids. They'll be spared a lot of grief if they stay true to their Savior. I envy their parents, too. By serving as godly role models for their children, they too will escape some heartaches.

All your parental duties point to one special day in the future—the day of your child's salvation. Don't believe those who will tell you that small children can't understand the gospel—young ones often understand it far better than we adults.

I know you're already praying for your baby. Make sure part of your prayers are focused on hastening that day of salvation. Let your conversation with your child include references to Christ and His love for your little one. At an early age, tell your son or daughter about the day you accepted Christ. Then one day, don't be surprised if that little one asks, "Dad, can I become a Christian too?"

Of all the joys a father can have—and we've mentioned a lot of them in these pages—by far the most rewarding is praying with your child to ask Christ into his or her heart. In the Old Testament it was dad's duty to circumcise the newborn son on the eighth day. In the New Testament, circumcision is "of the heart" (Romans 2:29), and represents the "born again" experience. Again, how appropriate for this to be dad's job...leading his child to Christ. Can you think of a greater pleasure?

Steve and I join you in praying for that day. May your little one soon be a child of the King.

Making It Happen—Read John 3:3-8. What did Jesus really mean in His explanation of the new birth to Nicodemus? How is being born physically similar to being born again spiritually?

Pass It On

One generation will commend your works to another;
they will tell of your mighty acts.

(PSALM 145:4)

If "Moses vs. the Pharaoh of Egypt" could have been seen on TV, you can bet the viewer ratings would have been off the charts. It's one thing to *read* about the ten plagues that God poured out upon the Egyptians, but imagine what it would have been like to *see* them! All ten plagues occurred in rapid succession. Each plague began instantaneously, took place on a massive scale, and ended instantaneously. These weren't the work of special-effects technicians; they were the real deal. Then they were followed by the parting of the Red Sea, a monumental miracle in its own right. And note that the people of Israel—an estimated two million strong—crossed through the sea on *dry* ground. When the Pharaoh's army gave chase, the Red Sea swallowed every last man—not one soldier survived (Exodus 14:28). Through all these events, the Israelites had witnessed a truly magnificent and extended display of God's power. This was the stuff of great stories for the grandchildren!

Considering the astounding magnitude of all that God had done, you would think the people of Israel had learned an unforgettable lesson. But just a few days into the wilderness journey, they were already grumbling that they had been led into the desert to die, and they wanted to return to Egypt. At Mount

Sinai, when Moses didn't return from the mountaintop right away, the people promptly created a god of their own to worship. Worst of all, when they reached the border of the Promised Land, fear paralyzed their hearts and they didn't battle for the land God had *promised* to give to them.

Were these really the same people who had seen all God's miracles in Egypt?

God knows how easily we are prone to forget the past. In Deuteronomy 6:7, we see Moses reminding the people of Israel to teach their children about God and His laws, and to "talk about them when you sit at home and when you walk along the road, when you lie down and when you get up." They were to make God known to their children at every opportunity. Sadly, in the centuries that followed, the parents in Israel neglected this duty, and the nation spiraled downward into spiritual decline and apostasy.

We who are Christian parents can learn from Israel's example. Psalm 145:4 calls one generation to proclaim God's goodness and mighty acts to the next so that no one will forget Him. We have the sacred privilege of impressing upon the minds and hearts of our children some of their earliest and most memorable lessons about God.

Making It Happen—Have you thought about how you can make God's work known to the next generation? As a father, that's one of your most important responsibilities. Take a moment now to commit yourself to making the most of this privilege. By proclaiming the praises of God to your children, you will teach them what great things the Lord can do, that He is intimately involved in our lives, and that He is worthy of our praise and adoration.

What's on the Menu?

The woman...nursed her son until she had weaned him.

(1 SAMUEL 1:23)

When should your baby make the transition to solid foods? Perhaps your parents and other relatives have already offered their thoughts on this. While opinions vary widely, most experts advise that the ideal age for making the change is four to six months. Your baby's digestive system needs time to mature. If you start too early, solid foods can end up passing through undigested, depriving your baby of the nutrients he or she needs.

Also, when you make the transition to solid foods, you're reducing the opportunities for the closeness and bonding that come with breast-feeding. Feel free, then, to spend a while alternating solid foods with breast-feeding so that the "cuddle times" aren't brought to an abrupt end. Another reason to continue the breast-feeding for at least a short while longer is that breast milk has nutrients that aren't readily replaced by solid foods.

When you make the changeover, your little one may take a while to adapt. He or she may find it hard to figure out how to get solids from the mouth to the throat. Your child may end up spitting the food out or contorting his or her face in bewilderment (be sure to have a camera or video camera handy—these facial expressions will be priceless!). Expect the transition to take some time. When your baby is hungry, start feeding him or her with solid food, and if you have little success, switch to breast-feeding or bottle-feeding. Your baby's receptivity to solid food will be greatest when he or she is hungriest. And if your child refuses to eat, you can then satisfy the hunger with breast or bottled milk.

When it comes to solid foods, single-grain baby cereals are a good place to start. You'll find rice, oatmeal, and barley cereals in boxes in the baby food section at your grocery store. If you want, you can add breast milk to the mix. When prepared, these cereals are almost liquid and are easy to swallow. They're also easy on the baby's digestive system and are among the least allergenic foods.

Before you add fruit juices to your baby's menu, be aware that their acidic content often leads to diarrhea or even allergic reactions. Fruit juices may also contribute to colic or restlessness. These are among the reasons the American Academy of Pediatrics recommends withholding fruit juice until six months of age. At first, fruit juices should be diluted 50/50 with water and served only occasionally.

Also, if you or your wife have a history of food allergies, you'll want to consult your pediatrician and get a list of foods to be wary of. *Always* call the pediatrician if your baby shows any kind of negative reaction to a food.

Finally, when you start your baby on solids, have him or her join you at the dining table in a high chair. This will help your child get used to your family's regular eating schedule.

Making It Happen—Buy one or two books that explain what to feed your baby and when. Do some research on the Internet as well. You'll discover a wide variety of advice, so it's best to become as well-informed as you can. Also, because every baby develops at a different pace, be flexible about how and when you make the transition to solid foods.

The End Result

...straining toward what is ahead,
I press on toward the goal.

(PHILIPPIANS 3:13-14)

Change the diaper. Warm a bottle of milk. Feed the baby. Burp the baby. Wash the bottle and dry it. Put the baby down for a nap. When baby wakes up and cries, change the diaper again. Dress the baby. Play with the baby. Warm another bottle of milk. Feed the baby again. And on and on it goes—in a seemingly endless cycle of repetition.

In the first year or two of fatherhood, you may have days when you feel as if being a dad is not a very high calling. At times you may feel as if you're merely a maintenance worker because the tasks are so basic and routine.

It's at times like these that it helps to keep the end result in mind. We are not just changing diapers and feeding, bathing, and clothing a helpless infant. We are nurturing and shaping a divinely created person who has the potential to someday serve God and bring glory to Him. We are raising up one who could have an active part in carrying on God's plan for the ages. And our influence on our child's life—beginning from day one—will significantly impact his or her desire to follow God and grow in godly character.

Because the early years of fatherhood are filled with seemingly mundane tasks, we can easily be tempted to do our work by rote, not putting our heart and soul into our everyday inter-action with our little one. We can fall into the trap of thinking that because babies understand so little, our job as fathers is merely functional.

But that's not true. The care and affection you take the time to communicate to your infant will definitely have a cumulative effect. The earlier you start and the more consistently you remember that you are producing a future servant of God, the more effective you will be in raising up your child in the ways of truth and righteousness.

Yes, you may still have hundreds more diapers to change. And hundreds more bottles to clean. (And when you think you're just about finished with this stage, your wife's pregnancy test will come back positive.) But in time, before you know it, God will begin to use your child's spiritual gifts and talents. And in God's kingdom, every hand counts. Every servant is of utmost importance, having a role to fill that was specially designated by no less than God Himself.

No task you do as a father is meaningless or trivial. You're raising a future servant of the King of the universe. That's a noble calling indeed!

Making It Happen—Read what 1 Corinthians 12:4-7 says about spiritual gifts. According to verse 7, who receives spiritual gifts? And what is their ultimate purpose? If your child becomes a Christian, he or she will become one of the unique and needed members of the body of Christ. So as you carry out the preparatory work you're doing today, remember to look ahead to the end result of your fathering efforts—you're preparing a future servant of the King of kings and Lord of lords.

Freedom from Bitterness

You have heard that it was said, "Love your neighbor and hate your enemy." But I tell you: Love your enemies and pray for those who persecute you.

(MATTHEW 5:43-44)

Have you ever noticed it's impossible to harbor bitterness toward a person and to truly love that person at the same time?

Through the years, I've observed this to be evident not only in the lives of people in general, but particularly among young couples who were going through a rocky patch in their marriage. Many of these husbands had developed an attitude of bitterness that was poisoning their marriage. Sometimes the bitterness was over the attention his wife was now giving to the baby instead of him. Other husbands were bitter about their in-laws, their own parents, or some other distraction that was robbing them and their wife of the satisfaction God had planned for their marriage.

How is it with you? Is there anything that is causing you to be bitter...or perhaps is just now surfacing that may lead to bitterness in the future?

What's scary about bitterness is the way it can spill over into our other relationships. Hebrews 12:15 says, "See to it...that no bitter root grows up to cause trouble and defile many." Bitterness is like an abscess in a tooth. Until the decaying matter is totally removed, the poison will continue to spread and destroy everything it touches.

When we sense bitterness arising within us—whether to our parents, in-laws, wife, or whoever—what can we do? Jesus gave a rather remarkable remedy in Matthew 5:44-45: "Love your enemies, bless those who curse you, do good to those who hate you, and pray for those who spitefully use you" (NKJV). Now, it's true Jesus is talking about those who do harm to us—in other words, someone else took the initiative to hurt us. In such cases, aren't we justified in taking corrective action? God gives us the answer in Romans 12:19: "Do not take revenge, my friends, but leave room for God's wrath, for it is written: 'It is mine to avenge; I will repay.'"

Usually when we're bitter it's because we've been wronged in some way. But that doesn't give us permission to hold on to negative feelings toward another person. As we just saw in Matthew 5:44-45, we're to love, bless, do good for, and pray for our enemies.

When you feel bitter, that's the remedy. Yes, it will be tough to let go of your anger. But with God's power and grace, you can do it. And in that same power and grace, you can love, bless, do good for, and pray for your enemies.

Are you bitter at someone now? During the next 30 days, pray for that person. Earnestly pray for his needs and for God's guidance in his life. Look for simple ways to affirm your care about him. Show deeds of kindness. And after 30 days, you're guaranteed to have a different perspective on that person—all because bitterness and love cannot reside in the same heart.

Making It Happen—Are you allowing the Prince of Peace to help bring peace to any bitter relationships in your life? Is there someone you can begin to love, bless, do good for, and pray for? Ask the Lord to help you apply Jesus' remedy and bring change to your heart. It will do a world of good for *all* your relationships, including the ones with those dearest to you—your wife and your children.

On the Road

Share with God's people who are in need.
Practice hospitality.

(Romans 12:13)

The first time I ever flew on a 747 Jumbo Jet, I sat in the center section. In the two seats to my left was a couple with an infant on their laps, and in the two seats to my right was *another* couple with an infant. Immediately I cringed at the thought that, during the flight, both babies might scream and cry—tantrums in stereo. But my concern wasn't so much for my own sanity; rather, I felt great sympathy for both sets of parents. I know how it feels to try to calm an upset baby when you're in a church service, a restaurant, or any place crowded with people. In most places, you can simply get up and leave. But an airplane is a bit different. You can't just step out the door for the sake of your fellow passengers.

Traveling with your baby doesn't need to be difficult. In fact, it can be surprisingly easy if you're fully prepared. Here are some tips to keep in mind:

Have your diaper bag stocked with a couple days' worth of the usual items—diapers, wipes, utensils, bottles, a soft blanket, extra outfits, a cloth diaper (for burps and cleanup), and a pacifier. Don't stock everything your baby is going to need for the entire trip—make your load lighter and buy supplies at stops along your travel route.

Use a separate backpack or duffle bag for your baby's "activity" items, such as toys, stuffed animals, and picture books. Bring along his or her favorite playthings so you can surround your child with familiar objects while in unfamiliar surroundings.

Invest in a light, collapsible playpen and stroller that are safe and takes up little space. You'll find these invaluable for use in hotel rooms and during walks or hikes.

Don't cut corners when you buy a car seat. Buy one that is comfortable and easy to use. You're going to use this seat a bazillion times before retiring it—get a good one.

Feed your baby the same foods he or she receives at home. This will help make your little one more comfortable, and he or she will be less likely to have negative stomach reactions.

When traveling by car, don't require your baby to sit in a car seat for extended periods of time. Take plenty of breaks and walk around at road stops. When you provide variety and entertainment, your baby is less likely to get fussy or bored.

Don't board an airplane early, and try to sit near the front so you can get off faster. The shorter you can keep your baby "cooped up," the better. Also, have a pacifier or bottle handy to help your baby with the air pressure changes during takeoff and landing. You can also ask your pediatrician for an infant version of Dramamine, which will help your baby to sleep through the flight.

Making It Happen—Plan ahead by asking yourself some questions about each part of your trip: Will this scare our baby? Will this cause discomfort? How can we keep our child occupied and content? By anticipating what might happen, you'll be better prepared…and have a much more enjoyable trip.

What Are You Taking to Heaven?

Do not store up for yourselves treasures on earth....
But store up for yourselves treasures in heaven.

(MATTHEW 6:19-20)

You've probably heard the maxim that when you die, you can't take anything with you. There's also the old joke that says you never see a U-Haul trailer behind a hearse.

But that's not quite accurate. There *is,* in fact, something you can take to heaven with you. Perhaps you think I'm about to mention spiritual riches, but no, that's not what I have in mind. I'm talking about something physical, something tangible, something you can see and touch.

Your children.

Someday when you're standing on heaven's shore, you will look all around you, and none of your belongings, accomplishments, or awards will count for anything. They won't be there. Anything that gives you reason to be proud in this life won't be around to show to God or impress anyone else in eternity.

Except your children. That is, if they show up in heaven.

Now, I'm not saying that your children's final destination rests completely on your shoulders. The Bible makes it clear that going to heaven or hell is an individual decision. Each and every person must make that choice for himself. However, there's no question that parents have by far the greatest influence on a young child's life.

Every newborn's future is, in a sense, a blank slate. You as a parent can help chart a course in life that leads to God, spiritual life, and blessings.

And the younger you start with your child, the better. If you're a dad of little influence and your child's slate stays blank for too long, others will all too gladly step in and chart courses that, most likely, lead anywhere but to God and spiritual truth.

The Bible tells us that children are a treasure from the Lord, entrusted to our care. We need to care for them with eternity in mind. The best way to do that is to make your relationship with God a real and active part of your life—so much so that your child can't miss it and wants to enjoy the same kind of relationship with God. In addition, Deuteronomy 6:7 calls parents to teach God's words to their offspring: "Impress them on your children...talk about them when you sit...when you walk...when you lie down...when you rise up." Make God real to your children in as many ways as possible.

We can be certain that one of the greatest thrills we'll ever experience in all eternity is our first day in heaven. And surely the *next* greatest joy will be to see our children in heaven with us.

Making It Happen—In Joshua 24:15 Joshua said, "As for me and my household, we will serve the LORD." Is your love and reverence for the Lord obvious in your home? Is it evident to your children, or will it be evident as they grow older? What are two or three things you can do as parents to make your love and service to the Lord more obvious in your home?

Your Uniqueness As a Dad

Then Nathan said to the king,
"Go, do all that is in your heart, for the LORD is with you."

(2 SAMUEL 7:3 NKJV)

No doubt you've been given lots of advice on fatherhood from many different sources. Even Steve and I—total strangers to you—have offered our perspective on fatherhood for your consideration. But as you wade through all the words of wisdom, remember this: God wants you to put *your* own unique spin on fatherhood by following your own paternal qualities and giftedness.

As time goes by, certain ways of doing things will occur to you. They may not be the way Steve would do it, or I would do it, or your dad did it. But in some special way, it's the way *you* do it.

Being a dad isn't simply following a bunch of dos and don'ts; it's much more creative than that. And you're a creative guy. As we've mentioned more than once, God has selected this child to be *your* child...and He's selected you to be this child's father. *You're the dad this child needs.* It's a great combination—literally birthed in heaven. And as you follow your paternal instincts, take the advice you get with a grain of salt, and place your full trust in God and His Word. With God's help, you just can't miss, so be confident!

Fatherhood is a new phase in your life (one of many to follow)—a phase in which you'll discover and use some gifts

God gave you long ago. Don't be afraid to be a dad *your* way—as long as everything you do respects the child as an individual and honors God and His Word.

There is a lot of room for variation in fatherhood. A lot of room for innovation. So go for it. Be the best. Be a great dad.

Making It Happen—See if you can list three things you're already doing as a father that are uniquely you—things you've not learned any-where else. If not, don't worry...they'll come. And when they do, take note that God is giving you personal insight as a father—give Him the credit, too!

1.

2.

3.

Appendix A

E–Z Diaper Folding

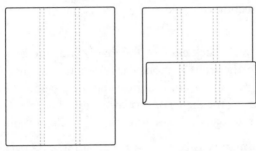

1. Prefold diaper. Dotted lines indicate thick center panel.

2. Fold up bottom third of diaper. For newborns, fold up bottom half, shortening fold as your baby grows.

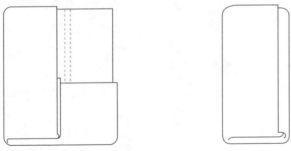

3. Fold left side panel over thick center panel.

4. Fold right side panel over, tucking it under the first folded side panel. This locks the sections together for a neater look and a better fit.

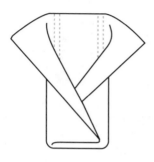 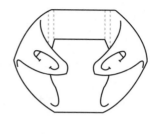

5. Open overlapping back section. Place baby on diaper with the wide top section centered at the baby's legs. Close in between the legs.

6. Bring the wide back ends of the diaper over the baby's hips and pin to the front section. Ease the pad section wider as necessary to comfortably encircle the baby below the navel. While pinning the diaper, insert your finger between the baby and diaper for baby's protection. Pin *out* as illustration shows.

This information is courtesy of the National Association of Diaper Services. Check out their website (www.diapernet.com) for lots of interesting information about diapers and newborns (they also illustrate a "no pins" diaper).

Appendix B

Recommended Resources

Books About Parenting and Family*

The Baby Book: Everything You Need to Know About Your Baby from Birth to Age Two by Dr. William and Martha Sears (Little, Brown and Co.)

The Complete Book of Christian Parenting & Childcare: A Medical & Moral Guide to Raising Happy, Healthy Children by Dr. William and Martha Sears (Broadman and Holman)

How to Raise Your Children for Christ by Andrew Murray (Bethany House Publishers)

Shepherding a Child's Heart by Tedd Tripp (Shepherd Publishers)

The Family by John F. MacArthur, Jr. (Moody Press)

10 Things I Want My Son to Know by Steve Chapman (Harvest House Publishers)

10 Things I Want My Daughter to Know by Annie Chapman (Harvest House Publishers)

The Focus on the Family Complete Book of Baby and Child Care (Tyndale House Publishers)

The New Dare to Discipline by James Dobson (Tyndale House Publishers)

Bringing Up Boys by James Dobson (Tyndale House Publishers)

A Full Quiver: Family Planning and the Lordship of Christ by Rick and Jan Hess (order from www.quiverfull.com)

* In the event that any of these books are out of print, check www.bookfinder.com on the Internet for a used copy.

The Family Bed by Tine Thevenin (Perigee Publishing)

The Mystery of Children by Mike Mason (Waterbrook Press)

The Power of a Praying Parent by Stormie Omartian (Harvest House Publishers)

How to Really Love Your Child by Ross Campbell (Chariot Victor Books)

Yes, They're All Ours: Six of One, Half a Dozen of the Other by Rick and Marilyn Boyer (The Learning Parent, Rustburg, Virginia)

Books About Godly Manhood

A Man After God's Own Heart by Jim George (Harvest House Publishers).

Disciplines of a Godly Man by R. Kent Hughes (Crossway Books)

Books to Read to Your Child

The New Bible in Pictures for Little Eyes by Kenneth N. Taylor (Moody Publishers)

A Child's Garden of Prayer by Steve and Becky Miller (Harvest House Publishers)

God's Wisdom for Little Boys—Character-Building Fun from Proverbs by Jim and Elizabeth George (Harvest House Publishers)

God's Wisdom for Little Girls—Virtues & Fun from Proverbs 31 by Elizabeth George (Harvest House Publishers)

Websites

Focus on the Family: www.family.org

National Fatherhood Initiative: www.fatherhood.org

Quiverfull.com: www.quiverfull.com

The Patriarch's Path: www.patriarchspath.org

National Center for Fathering: www.fathers.com

Men's Fraternity: www.mensfraternity.com

Promise Keepers: www.promisekeepers.org

Subject Index

—ᴠᴠ—

Notes

1. Article on Internet, "High Prices in London for Picasso and Monet," at www.senrs.com/high_prices_in_london_for_ picasso_and_monet.htm.

2. Ibid.

3. Article on Internet, "Record Price for Cezanne," at http://www.artcult.com/news15m.htm.

4. Joseph A. Breig, *A Halo for Father* (Milwaukee, WI: The Bruce Publishing Company, 1953), pp. 72-74.

5. Larry Burkett, *The Complete Financial Guide for Young Couples: A Lifetime Approach to Spending, Saving and Earning* (Colorado Springs: Cook Communications Ministries, 1989), p. 11.

6. Frank Batten, *The Weather Channel* (Boston, MA: Harvard Business School Press, 2002), p. 3.

7. Ibid., p. 50.

8. Margaret J. Preston, "General Lee After the War," in *The Century* (New York: The Century Company, 1889), vol. 38, issue 2, p. 276.

9. *Marriage Partnership* magazine, Summer 1997, p. 46.